Easy Peasy
FRENCH
BULLDOG

Also by Steve Mann:

Easy Peasy Puppy Squeezy

Easy Peasy Doggy Squeezy

Easy Peasy Doggy Diary

Easy Peasy Awesome Pawsome

Easy Peasy Labrador

Easy Peasy Labradoodle

Easy Peasy Cockapoo

Easy Peasy Cocker Spaniel

Easy Peasy
FRENCH BULLDOG

Your Simple Step-By-Step Guide to
Raising and Training a Happy French Bulldog

STEVE MANN

With Martin Roach

Layout Design: Envy Design Ltd
All photographs © Dan Rouse
All illustrations © Shutterstock

For permission requests, please contact the publisher at:
Mango Publishing Group
2850 S Douglas Road, 2nd Floor
Coral Gables, FL 33134 USA
info@mango.bz

For special orders, quantity sales, course adoptions and corporate sales, please email the publisher at sales@mango.bz. For trade and wholesale sales, please contact Ingram Publisher Services at customer.service@ingramcontent.com or +1.800.509.4887.

Easy Peasy French Bulldog: Your Simple Step-By-Step Guide to Raising and Training a Happy French Bulldog

Library of Congress Cataloging-in-Publication number: has been requested
ISBN: (pb) 978-1-68481-506-7 (e) 978-1-68481-507-4
BISAC: PET004020, PETS / Dogs / Training & Showing

This book is dedicated to those that are committed to
giving dogs the happiest and healthiest life possible

A Note About French Bulldogs

It may well be that your heart is set on a French Bulldog, or even that you are already a proud owner of one – however, I cannot stress enough the health implications, distress and concerns that can be caused by poor breeding of French Bulldogs. Please, please, *please*, if Frenchies are for you, please insist on the very highest standards of health and breeding when you make your choice.

CONTENTS

ABOUT THE AUTHOR

Steve Mann, founder of the IMDT (Institute of Modern Dog Trainers), is the author of the UK's number 1 bestselling dog training book *Easy Peasy Puppy Squeezy*. Other books include the bestselling *Easy Peasy Doggy Squeezy*, *Easy Peasy Doggy Diary* and *Easy Peasy Awesome Pawsome*.

Steve is a world-renowned expert who presents dog training and behaviour seminars worldwide including Europe, South America, Africa and the Middle East. TV appearances include BBC's *The Underdog Show* and *Who Let The Dogs Out?*, ITV's *Lorraine* and *Animal Rescue*, plus several other shows in the UK and worldwide. Steve has worked with many celebrities including Graham Norton, Brian Blessed and Theo Walcott. He also works as an animal consultant for TV and film shoots and regularly speaks at behaviour, management and training conferences.

You can find out more at www.stevemanndogtraining.com and www.imdt.uk.com.

FRENCH BULLDOGS: THE STATS

🐾 **DOG TYPE:** Utility/Non-Sporting

🐾 **SIZE:** Small

🐾 **AVERAGE LIFE EXPECTANCY:**
Over 10 years

🐾 **COAT:** Short, sheds

🐾 **HEIGHT:** Around 28–30cm for males;
similar for females

🐾 **WEIGHT:** Ideally no more than 28lb for males;
around 24lb for females

INTRODUCTION

So, you're a fan of the pocket rocket known as the French Bulldog, eh?

I don't blame you, they're a huge amount of fun in a small package and as long as we can keep them healthy, they're fantastic companions that love and live life to the full!

One of the very first dogs that got me obsessed with dog training many years ago as a kid was a neighbour's little fawn French Bulldog named Pierre. I used to knock on my neighbour's door to see if 'Pierre could come out to play?' – the same way other kids would knock for their *human* friends to come out to play! Pierre was so typical of the breed: always up for a game, always happy to have new adventures, and always happy to bite and shake the living daylights out of any new toys I could make or find for him!

French Bulldogs make for good dog trainers. By that, I mean the skill of a dog trainer is to recognise what your chosen breed is hard-wired to love doing, and to use those fun activities to exchange for the behaviours you want more of.

If you try to block and supress your French Bulldog from exercising the skills of chasing and grabbing (which were so useful in the olden days when rat-catchers were most welcome in the factory and household), you'll find your daily life feeling like trying to screw the lid back onto a very fizzy bottle of cola! You'll end up with a dog that doesn't look to you to get their joy, instead they will choose to go 'self-employed' (I'll explain that concept a bit more later)!

However, if YOU become the source of joy for your Frenchie by producing magnificent toys for them to chase and grab – not only will YOU be the centre of attention and the source of great fun which your dog will love you for, but you'll build up a fantastic treasure trove of activities and games to exchange for the behaviours you want more of, such as a speedy Recall at the local park!

French Bulldogs are amazing dogs that really wear their hearts on their sleeves and return the love and affection of their human family ten-fold.

Now, I'm a professional dog trainer by trade, so you will find a lot of tips and insider info in this book about how to best train your fantastic French Bulldog. However, training your Frenchie is only a fraction of the responsibility you have for your dog, so within these pages I want to help you through all of the potential twists and turns that you'll hit as a proud dog owner. We're going to make sure you're happy, confident and fully equipped with a broad and well-balanced knowledge of French Bulldogs – from choosing the right dog for you, toilet training, diet and grooming to discovering what activities your dog will love (and hate!), appropriate exercise routines and, of course, how to teach the essential skills such as Loose Lead Walking and Recall. All of this will make your life with your French Bulldog as fun and rewarding as possible.

Enjoy this book, keep your dog happy and healthy, and I wish you many years of fantastic Frenchie adventures ahead...

Bon chance!

Steve Mann

FRENCH BULLDOGS – WHERE IT ALL BEGAN...

So, believe it or not, your little French Bulldog, known in some circles as 'a bowling ball of a dog', has a history and backstory that takes in Sherwood Forest, the Industrial Revolution, Bohemian nineteenth-century Paris as well as artists such as Toulouse-Lautrec and even Russian royalty!

Jump in a time-machine and travel back to the late eighteenth and early nineteenth centuries and you will be hard pushed to find another dog breed that was back then, and remains to this day, one of the dog-loving world's absolute favourites.

That's where we will find out more about the ancestry of

this fantastic little breed. With the advancing technological innovation of the Industrial Revolution accelerating at pace, the story turns to Nottingham in the English Midlands – home to Robin Hood and Sherwood Forest. Here, in the cramped, dangerous and gruelling factories that paid their workers low wages while making high profits, there was a local population of lacemakers, struggling to get by on their meagre incomes. These skilled women had a fashion for taking diminutive English Toy Bulldogs to work with them – some historians think this is because the dogs were small enough to keep them company in the limited workspaces, and possibly even sat on their laps. Regardless of how unpleasant or decrepit these factories were, this was still a far more preferable life for these little dogs than the fate that often awaited their more traditional larger Bulldog counterparts, who very often endured a life of blood sports and horrific violence.

Unfortunately, the days of these dog-loving lacemakers were numbered. With innovation continuing apace, the majority soon found themselves out of work and instead headed across the English Channel to the Normandy region of northern France. The Gallic obsession with beautifully made clothes was still very much in vogue, so the lacemakers found work and a warm welcome ... as did their mild-mannered, small Bulldogs. These English Toy Bulldogs evidently bred with some native terriers and that is how we first began to see the origins of your delightful little Frenchie. The exporting of Bulldogs that were considered 'too small' from the UK to France quickly ramped up and included dogs who had less traditional physical attributes – such as most obviously ears that stood upright, rather than the more common 'rose' ear of the bigger English Bulldog.

In no time at all, these completely charming and loveable little Bulldogs became popular across many levels of French society, including in the capital where they could be found frequenting the artists' studios, late-night restaurants and coffee bars of the Parisian district of Montmartre. In fact, these little Bulldogs started to appear everywhere – even in brothels! Indeed, Bulldog folklore tells of one such dog who was in the habit of wee-ing on the feet of any of his lady owner's 'patrons' who tried to fuss him! Over the coming years, these stubby-faced little dogs became so well known that some of them even started to appear on risqué postcards with 'ladies of the night'! By sharp contrast, the artists Edgar Degas and Toulouse-Lautrec both featured French Bulldogs in a number of their paintings.

The breed's popularity continued to spread fast, soon leading to its own breed name: *Bouledogue Francais* (*boule* – ball; *dogue* – mastiff). The Grand Duchess Tatiana Romanov of Russian royalty had a Frenchie called Ortipo – sadly, neither the dog nor the owner survived the approaching

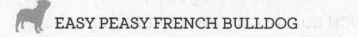

revolution. A similar premature end befell the magnificently named Gamin de Pycombe, whose doting wealthy banker owner took him on the ill-fated *Titanic*. The owner survived; sadly the dog, which had cost £150 (a five-figure sum today), did not make it home.

The breed soon exploded in popularity in the United States, where Frenchie lovers founded the very first club specifically for French Bulldogs and their owners. This group of women created the breed standard in the last few years of the 1800s, and included in that description the 'erect bat ear' as the 'correct' type. In 1905, the Kennel Club in the UK also recognised the French Bulldog as a separate breed in its own right.

During a lull in the difficult pre- and post-Second World War years, certain countries classified the Frenchie as a 'rare breed', but by the 1980s the dog's popularity began to re-ignite. Celebrities and high society adopted the dog, as did generations of dog-lovers around the globe – smitten by the breed's heart-warming companionship, fun-loving nature and gentle, loyal personality. In the social media age, the French Bulldog is one of the most visible and cherished breeds in the world. So, when you cuddle or play with your own adorable Frenchie – just remember, they have a very colourful and fascinating past!

10 FUN FACTS ABOUT FRENCH BULLDOGS

1. Due to their squat build and large, round head, most Frenchies can't swim!

2. After a few Frenchies experienced breathing difficulties in pressurised airplane cabins, a dedicated airline started transporting dogs with such special needs: PetJets!

3. A nine-year-old French Bulldog called Bugsy became best friends with an orangutan that had been abandoned at a zoo – they even had sleepovers.

4. Celebrities such as Lady Gaga, The Rock, Leonardo Di Caprio and Hugh Jackman are all besotted French Bulldog owners.

5. French Bulldogs don't actually originate from France – an English artisan in Nottingham gave the dogs their name after breeding began in France.

6. Frenchies can out-fart most dogs, so much so that there are even 'Anti-Fart Dog Biscuits' for the stinky puppers!

7. Some people call them 'Clown Dogs' due to their fun-loving and, at times, comedic nature.

8. The top five most popular names for French Bulldogs are Lola, Louie, Stella, Bella and Luna.

9. In the 1930s, the owners of a French Bulldog called Princess Jacqueline claimed their dog could 'speak' 20 words!

10. The American Kennel Club states that, for their purposes, there are nine colours of French Bulldog, including brindle, fawn and cream.

HOW TO SPOT A
GOOD BREEDER

If you plan on getting a French Bulldog puppy from a breeder, believe me, it's one of the biggest commitments you're ever going to make in your life. Get it right, and your puppy – and eventually your adult dog – will bring a huge amount of joy to your life over many years. Get it wrong, and the stresses, concerns and heartache may be unbearable for you ... and for the dog.

Let's have a look at a few tips on how to spot a good breeder, and when to 'vote with your feet' by walking away from the wrong 'uns. Before we do, bear in mind that a good breeder who cares for their pups will welcome as many questions as you can throw at them, they'll be delighted to answer any and all queries, and they'll be proud to think that their pup is going to someone that cares enough to do thorough due diligence. A bad breeder will avoid questions and not want to give comprehensive answers. Let that be your first clue!

First things first, before we even consider the important character and formative mental development of your French Bulldog pup through early, careful and considerate exposure to their new world, let's make sure this puppy has the best chance of being physically healthy by ensuring that you can see the certified evidence that both of their parents have been tested, and passed with flying colours, for:

Healthy eyes: Both parents should be Eye Screened and certificates are to be supplied by the breeder to verify that there are no eye issues, including the absence of cataracts.

Degenerative Myelopathy: A disorder affecting the spinal cord tissues, resulting in the ability to walk being impaired.

Congenital Hypothyroidism: A condition associated with abnormal thyroid development, causing delayed growth and development (dwarfism).

Hyperuricosuria: A painful condition resulting in a build-up of crystals in the urinary tract, caused by high levels of uric acid in the urine.

In addition to the above formal tests that must be carried out by the breeder, I want you to promise me here and now that you'll see both parents and if you have **any** concerns – even if it's just a gut-feeling that either of the parents may have skin issues, breathing difficulties, a very flat face, prominent eyes or that their teeth look really closely packed in their mouth, please, I beg you, say, 'Thanks, but no thanks', and walk away. It may be tough in the moment, but for the benefit of the French Bulldog as a breed, and the benefit of dogs in general, we can't support inconsiderate breeding.

Once you're confident that the above physical disadvantages have been successfully ruled out of the litter you're considering, we can move on to the other factors we need to be satisfied with to ensure the best start possible is being given to your *potential* new pup. I say potential because, as hard as it seems, I STILL need you to be thinking with your head, and not *yet* with your heart ...

So here are some golden rules for this very important decision:

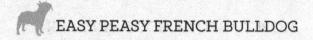

Can you see the litter at home, with their mother, in the area they've been raised in?

It's important you can see the rearing area so you can make sure it's not only safe and clean, but also that it's a nice, busy area with plenty of hustle and bustle. Despite what many first-time puppy owners might think, we don't want litters that are reared in a quiet, secluded area. We want a litter that sees LOTS of day-to-day goings-on: TVs, people, radio, doors closing, laughing, kids, other pets, visitors ... and so on. An area such as a busy household kitchen is great because the pups can naturally absorb that essential exposure to the world *as soon as possible*. The more sights, sounds, smells (within reason!) and textures the pups can be exposed to, as early as possible, the better chance those pups will have to become well-rounded and well-socialised dogs in the future.

If for some reason you're not permitted to see the area, then simply say, 'Thanks, but no thanks'.

If the area is too quiet and secluded, same again, 'Thanks, but no thanks'.

If the breeder suggests you meet in a neutral venue, 'to save travel' ... 'Thanks, but no thanks'.

When you see the mother of the litter, ensure she's friendly and confident. If you can't see the mother – even if you're told by the breeder that 'She ... er, is just out walking at present', say, 'Thanks, but no thanks'. Same response if the mother lacks confidence or is neither friendly nor happy to see you.

If you suspect (and believe me, this happens), that the bitch you're being told is the mother may not actually be the mother, this is obviously a big red flag, so walk away.

What socialisation has the breeder completed with the pups?
The pups need to be safely seeing, hearing, smelling and touching as many things as possible, so they can start to build a nice robust, optimistic and confident association to the world around them.

Is each puppy getting lots of individual attention and handling?
It's important that each puppy has the opportunity to become happy about being handled away from the rest of the litter, to build confidence and to create a positive relationship with humans.

Do the puppies look healthy and happy?
Sounds obvious but your gut feeling here will be pretty accurate. If in doubt, please take an experienced dog owner with you to ensure there's no redness, soreness, lameness or other signs of stress.

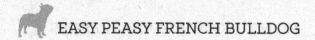 EASY PEASY FRENCH BULLDOG

Are the puppies fed a healthy diet, and how are they fed?

To give them the best start in life, it's important the pups are fed a healthy, well-balanced diet, not just some cheap supermarket junk food.

Crucially, ask not only *what* they're fed, but also, *how* are they fed?

Rather than all the pups eating from the same large bowl, which will only encourage in-fighting, food guarding and panic at mealtimes, I'd much rather each pup was fed from an individual bowl. Even better than that, I'd like each puppy to eat from an individual bowl in their own crate or den. Not only will they love their food, but they'll also learn to love being in their den due to the positive association at mealtimes. A puppy that goes to their new home already loving their den will really excel at night-time routines, toilet training and the prevention of separation anxiety. What a huge advantage to the puppy and new owner, for such a small effort from the breeder!

Has toilet training started for the litter yet?

From the age of three to four weeks, *given the chance*, puppies will move away from the sleeping and playing area of the den to eliminate (i.e. go to the loo). Make sure the breeder has encouraged and reinforced this natural impulse by providing a clearly designated toileting area, ideally laying the area with soil or grass, because ultimately that's where you'd like the puppy to go pee-pees!

What constructive activities does the breeder do with each puppy?

When you ask this question, leave it fairly open-ended, so the breeder can elaborate. You never know, you may be surprised! I'd be hoping the breeder will be doing things along the lines of: introducing grooming brushes; handling routines such as ear cleaning; introducing hand-feeding to help with future training; or even pairing a whistle to treats as a foundation to teaching Recall.

Other things the breeder should be doing on an individual basis is something us dog trainers like to call Early Neurological Stimulation (ENS). It sounds technical, but it's essentially a gentle way to kick-start the puppy's neurological systems and therefore should be performed once a day between the ages of three to 16 days.

Each of the five ENS exercise takes only three to five seconds and for a daily time cost of 25 seconds per pup, the recorded benefits of ENS include a greater tolerance to stress later in life, as well as a greater resistance to disease. Not a bad investment, eh?

These five daily ENS exercises comprise:

1. Tactile Stimulation: Hold the pup with one hand and gently touch between their toes with a cotton bud.
2. Head Held Erect: Gently hold the pup vertical, head directly above butt.
3. Head Held Low: VERY gently hold the pup vertically with two hands, head down, butt in the air.
4. Supine: Gently cradle the puppy on their back in your two hands, like they're in a hammock facing upwards!
5. Thermal Stimulation: Pop the puppy onto a damp tea cloth or towel. The cool water on the towel will automatically alert the pup to the shift in temperature (if the puppy tries to move off the towel, that's fine, do not restrain them).

My advice is most definitely go to a breeder that knows, understands and performs ENS for their puppies.

Other red flags to suggest a 'Thanks, but no thanks' include:

🐾 The breeder seems more interested in money than the pup's potential home.

- The breeder doesn't know a lot about the breed.
- The breeder has bred several litters of differing breeds.
- The breeder doesn't like you asking questions.
- The breeder has no medical records showing clear health results of the parents.
- The breeder does not offer a lifetime return policy; they should always be willing to take the puppy back if things don't work out.

BRACHYCEPHALIC

The word Brachycephalic originates from two Greek words meaning 'short' and 'head'. A French Bulldog is a brachycephalic breed, which means they are bred to have a flattened face and muzzle.

Sadly, as with many breeds, certain physical characteristics are exaggerated through breeding – often at the expense of both the breed and of the individual dog. When the shortening of the muzzle is taken to extremes, the dog can suffer the consequences with issues such as breathing problems, also known as 'BOAS' – Brachycephalic Obstructive Airway Syndrome or brachycephalic syndrome. This issue is seen with far too many short-faced dogs.

Through bad breeding, the windpipe of a brachy-cephalic dog can be deformed and too narrow – restricting the amount of air that can flow, which not only affects breathing but can also lead to heart problems.

Surely an ability to breathe comfortably is the bare minimum all dogs should be permitted?!

Sadly, brachycephalic breeds are more likely to overheat in hot weather due to their inability to efficiently pant – a restriction also caused by their shorter muzzle.

I appreciate that that's all pretty tough reading, so let's see how we can find some positives for you.

If you're thinking of getting a French Bulldog, the responsibility is on you to do your due diligence and to *always* have the dog's health at heart. You MUST make sure you go to a breeder who has the dog's, and the breed's, health and welfare as their number one priority.

Ensure that the puppy's parents have had all the relevant health tests and make sure you can see the original vet certificates to support that claim. Don't be afraid to contact the vet in question to check – this is your dog's life at stake, so leave no stone unturned.

If the breeder is wary or not happy with you putting the dog's welfare front and centre, then move on ... they're not the right breeder for you.

When looking at the parents of the litter, I want you to only consider a pup from parents that have 'longer than average' muzzles.

If you already have your French Bulldog, to help navigate

potential brachycephalic problems, please make sure your dog is not overweight and ensure they are well protected in warmer weather.

I want you to do the very best for yourself and your French Bulldog in general here, so I absolutely appreciate that I've laid down some strict ground rules for you. However, until breeders realise that owners demand the best standards and that the days of 'good enough is good enough' are no longer acceptable, then standards won't improve.

It's too important to cut corners or to take a risk; let's all do the very best we can for our French Bulldogs.

Don't give in to sales pressure and be strong enough to think beyond the puppy's adorable cuteness.

If the cost of getting a healthy, happy family member is merely asking a few extra awkward questions, then so be it – be brave!

THE RESCUE
FRENCH BULLDOG

I've always had rescue dogs and although I must admit it gives me a nice warm fuzzy feeling in my tummy to know that I've given a home to a previously abandoned dog, I'm no Saint Steve of Assisi. The truth is, in many ways, taking on a rescue dog is often much easier than taking on a puppy.

With a dog taken on from a good rescue centre, you'll have the luxury of time to enjoy multiple visits to get to know that particular French Bulldog, finding out about their individual personality, what training exercises you can prioritise to make the transition into your home go nice and smoothly, and maybe go out to a few different locations and environments to make sure you suit, accommodate and satisfy each other's needs. It's kinda like having a few dates before you get married, rather than one of those 'married at first sight' horror stories!

So, if you are going down the rescue route, here are a few pointers:

- 🐾 Be prepared: a good rescue centre will ask you a LOT of questions, it's only because they care!

- 🐾 Be honest with your answers: it's important for both you and the dog that you're a good match. Of course, as with all dogs including puppies 'straight out of the packet', you'll have work to do to round off a few edges with love, time and positive training. However, we don't want anyone to bite off more than they can chew, resulting in the poor dog bouncing around in the rescue system again.

Sometimes when people consider or take on a rescue dog, they almost assume the dog must have a kennel-load of emotional baggage due to being put up for adoption. Not necessarily, my friend!

Such assumptions can become as much of an obstacle to the dog's progress as inappropriate or excessive 'cotton-wool-wrapping-up' can hold the dog and owner back from enjoying life to the full.

Of course, listen to the rescue centre's advice and take the dog's history on board. If a little assistance is needed to help the dog feel better about certain situations or if they could do with some extra training to make life easier, then enlist the help of a professional dog trainer to do the work once and do it properly.

My advice to owners that take on a rescue dog is to go nice and steady for the first two or three weeks. As tempting as it is, don't have too many crazy adventures. Spend time setting up a nice secure and safe foundation, so that your new dog realises that 'this' is their new forever home. You want them to know that there's no rush ... that ultimately they get to spend the rest of their new beautiful life with their new beautiful hero – you.

EQUIPMENT

Back in the day, when I was a lowly 15-year-old apprentice dog trainer, I remember excitedly going to a working dog show to buy my first tracking harness. Now, for 'apprentice dog trainer' look up 'skint', 'poor' or 'penniless' in the dictionary and you won't be far off the truth.

As I fiddled with the sweaty pound notes in my pocket, I looked along the dog training equipment stall, picked up a beautiful handmade leather harness with brass buckles that was super-expensive, but perfect. The vendor watched me slowly put it down and then quickly pick up a cheaper nylon harness that'd do the job, but it wasn't *the one*.

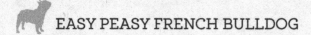

'This one please,' I said, as I handed the nylon harness to the salesman.

'Sure?' he said.

'Sure.'

'Okay, but if you buy cheap, you'll get cheap. If I were you, I'd buy once and buy properly.'

Damn! He had me.

'In fact, no ... this one please,' I said and quickly disregarded the nylon harness and slowly picked up the beautiful handmade harness with two hands, like I was handing a new-born to a radiant mother for the first time!

'Good man,' the stall holder said. 'Tell you what, you can have it for the same price as the nylon one. Good luck!'

Man alive! What a lesson and what a harness.

That was 35 years ago and I still have and love that harness to this day. It's been worn by many of my wonderful dogs over that time, trapping hundreds of amazing memories within its material and, do you know what? I wouldn't swap it for the world.

I guess what I'm saying is, when it comes to dog kit, do what the stall holder told me all those years ago: 'Buy once and buy properly.'

COLLAR

Comfort and safety are everything.

Your dog's collar should fit well. It should be loose enough that you can comfortably slide two fingers between the collar and your dog, but secure enough that it can't slip over your dog's head. A nice broad, flat buckle collar will do just the job.

HARNESS

When I'm out walking my dogs, for their comfort I prefer a well-fitting harness, rather than attaching the lead to their collar. Your dog's harness should allow free movement of their legs and shoulders, and not restrict any natural movement at all.

LEAD

To allow the lead to remain as slack as possible to encourage Loose Lead Walking (see page 81), I recommend a lead that is approximately two metres in length to allow your dog to sniff and avoid being restrained or restricted by the lead being too tight. Choose a material that's comfortable, strong and long-lasting. I'll leave the colour choice to you! (Although I like orange, as it is harder to lose.)

DEN

If you've got yourself a beautiful French Bulldog puppy, I'd recommend investing in a den which is simply a safe area that you can easily create with a foldable puppy pen. The den will help you create a safe space for your puppy's eating and sleeping, as well as protecting your carpet from piddles and your furniture from nibbles when you're not on guard!

BOWLS

For feeding and water, I like to use heavy porcelain bowls, as a lighter bowl can often start at one corner of the kitchen and end up on the other side of the room after a typical Frenchie feeding frenzy!

LONG LINE

A long line is a five- or 10-metre line that you can attach to your dog's harness when you're out and about; it allows for plenty of freedom, but gives you an added insurance and peace of mind that you can keep your dog safe and out of trouble. It's a really handy piece of kit to use as you're progressing through your Recall practice (see page 75), particularly if you're in an area that's not well enclosed, or in a location that's inhabited by wildlife or livestock.

POO BAGS

Don't leave home without them! Don't forget, kids, ensure your poo bags are plastic-free and biodegradable; we want future generations to enjoy poo-picking just as much as you and me!

TOYS

Playing with your dog is one of the real joys of living with canine companions. I always recommend that when buying any toys, you get two of the same. That way, when you throw toy #1 for your dog to go chase, as soon as they pick it up, you can then produce the identical toy #2 from your back pocket to encourage them back to you. As soon as they return to you and drop toy #1 ... you've guessed it ... throw toy #2 for them to go chase, as you pick up the dropped toy #1. Rinse and repeat as necessary.

Think about how your dog plays: if they love to chase, use balls; if they love to tug, a couple of knotted tea towels will be just the ticket.

Many French Bulldogs love to go 'all in' when they play, so whatever toys you choose, make sure they're robust!

PRINCIPLES OF TRAINING

I want to share with you my principles of dog training that will apply for all behaviours you want your dog to do, and maybe more importantly, all the behaviours you don't want your dog to do.

Some people don't like to admit it, but dogs are just like us! Okay, I admit they may have different toilet habits and sometimes their personal hygiene may leave a bit to be desired, but when it comes to how they learn and why they do the behaviours they do, us humans and canines are peas in a pod. Like us, dogs do behaviours that *work*.

Now, from a dog's perspective, behaviour is behaviour. It either serves a purpose or it doesn't. When we study

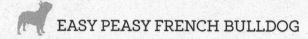

behaviour, there's no moral compass differentiating between *good* behaviour and *bad* behaviour – simply behaviour that's worth doing, and behaviour that isn't.

If your dog does a behaviour that you'd like more of, such as sitting to say, 'Hi' to visitors or coming when called, ensure you make that behaviour worth doing again in the future by reinforcing it with a treat, a fuss or a play – whatever your dog most enjoys at that time.

1. **Be Generous With Your Feedback**
   I have a saying that I often use: *what gets treated gets repeated.* So be generous with your feedback to your Frenchie because, let's face it, if you receive something wonderful for doing a particular behaviour, I'd be pretty damn confident you'd be more likely to repeat that behaviour in the future!

   Giving your dog something they enjoy as a consequence of the behaviour they've just done – whether you asked for it or not – is known in dog training circles as 'positive reinforcement'.

2. **Have Realistic Expectations**
   When training, make sure you have realistic expectations!
   The name of the game is to achieve as much

success as possible, so you can reinforce as much as possible. This reinforcement will then make the behaviours you want become as reliable as possible!

Sounds easy, doesn't it?

Well, it is (even I can do it!), as long as you're not too greedy with what you're asking for.

When you start any exercise, go very slowly and set a nice, low criteria for your dog to meet, so you can both be happy by avoiding frustration. Let's use 'Down' as an example:

From a 'Sit' position, take a treat and lure your dog's head down between their feet then along the floor until they flatten out to let their chest touch the floor. Once in a Down position, give them the treat to reinforce the behaviour of following the lure into a Down position.

As with all training at all levels, make sure the environment and surface are as comfortable as possible; no Frenchie in their right mind wants to lay down on a hard, cold, wet surface!

The next stage is to add the cue 'Down' as your dog goes into the correct position. Again, treat each time they do to *reinforce* the behaviour, to make it more reliable and robust for the next repetition.

47

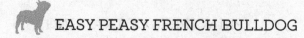

EASY PEASY FRENCH BULLDOG

Once your dog is smoothly and reliably going into a Down position on the verbal cue, you can start raising the criteria with your three Ds.

3. **The 3Ds: Duration, Distance and Distraction**
To begin with, set a nice achievable bar so your dog can hit the desired criteria to earn reinforcement. However, once the behaviour is ESTABLISHED, we can raise the bar by increasing what I call 'The 3Ds':

For example, successfully ask your dog to do a Down, then increase the *Duration* from one second, to three seconds of them being in position before saying, 'Good' as you give them the treat. If that's successful, aim for five seconds, ten seconds and so on.

To raise the *Distance* criteria, ask your dog to go into a Down, then take a step away from them, before returning and saying, 'Good' and treating. Successful? Great! Aim for two steps for the next repetition, then three, then four...

Remember, we said to have *realistic* expectations? So, if your dog is a little wobbly or not nailing 10 out of 10 for two steps away, then don't try and aim for more than three steps. Therein lies disaster!

Make sure you can get 10 out of 10 for any criteria shift before raising the bar. Slowly, slowly catchy monkey!

Our final criteria shift, *Distraction*, is where you can start acting the clown!

Ask for a Down, then you can start to hop on one foot two or three times, or pat your head and rub your tummy. If your dog remains in a Down, even though you've started to act a little weird, then go back to them, say, 'Good' and treat. If your movements proved too distracting this time, no worries at all, just lower the criteria and reduce your movements for the next repetition – get success and build on from there.

Remember: there's no such thing as failure in dog training, only *feedback*. The skill of a dog trainer is to take that feedback and to *make a change to make a change*.

No matter what you're teaching – Loose Lead Walking, Recall, Sit, etc. – the rules of the 3Ds remain the same: set realistic expectations, practise in a comfortable area, and raise or lower your Duration, Distance and Distractions as appropriate to ensure the flow of positive reinforcement remains high.

4. **Proofing**

   Once you've nailed a behaviour in a particular environment, start to practise and rehearse in a variety of locations. This change of locations is called *proofing* a behaviour and is the most reliable way to ensure your training exercises remain as robust as possible.

5. **To punish or not?**

   'Positive reinforcement is all very well for the behaviours I <u>do</u> want,' I hear you say, '... but what about the behaviours I <u>don't</u> want!?'

   Fair point!

   So, here's the plan. We're not going to look to <u>punish</u> *bad* behaviours.

   Remember, for us behaviourists, there's no such thing as bad behaviour – only behaviour that works ... and behaviour that doesn't.

   You'll have noticed that by using positive reinforcement for our Down training, you'll emerge from the session feeling happy and relaxed. This is because by setting appropriate criteria, you'll have put yourself in a position to recognise and treat your dog for getting it *right* many times over. Not only will you feel good about the session and your dog, but your dog will also emerge feeling good about the session, looking forward to the next one and loving you. Everyone's happy!

Let's say you made the HUGE mistake of punishing your dog each time they weren't successful. Not only will you finish the session unhappy and tense, but your dog will also emerge feeling bad about the session, not looking forward to the next one and fearing you. Nobody's happy!

For unwanted behaviours – such as chewing, toileting mistakes, jumping up at visitors, running away at the park etc. – let's get smart.

We're not going to use punishment – we're not bullies. No, instead we're going to use what is called 'Control and Management' as well as 'Mutually Exclusive Behaviours'.

6. **Control and Management**
Sounds a bit scientific – and it is – but essentially this just means that with your super-intelligent brain you're going to control the environment, so your dog is unable to practise, and therefore inadvertently be rewarded for doing, any unwanted behaviour.

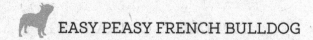

Remember, living with a dog can be tricky because you're not the only one that's able to reward behaviour. Damn! Even unwanted behaviour can be rewarded, such as the pain relief gained by the teething puppy chewing the furniture, the bladder relief of peeing on the carpet, or the sheer joy of interacting with a child gained through jumping up at them to *insist* on interaction!

With the careful use of Control and Management, we can save the chewing of the furniture by not allowing your puppy in the living room unattended. We can keep the carpet clean with the use of a puppy den when your puppy is left unattended and we can stop your dog ambushing children at the park by keeping them on the lead or long line.

7. **Mutually Exclusive Behaviours**

Control and Management is only half of the story though. It's one thing to stop your dog from doing the unwanted behaviour, but that only creates a bit of a vacuum. The follow-up question must always be, 'What do we want them to do *instead*?'

The 'instead' behaviour is called the Mutually Exclusive Behaviour. Essentially, if your dog is doing the Mutually Exclusive Behaviour, then they can't be doing the unwanted behaviour at the same time.

The trick is to make the alternative Mutually Exclusive Behaviour as <u>reinforcing as possible</u> in the scenarios where the unwanted behaviour used to previously occur.

For example, when in the living room with your teething pup, rather than their eye wandering over to the legs of the dining table, make sure they have lots of attractive alternative chews for pain relief and to keep them occupied. After all, they can't chew their favourite stuffed toy AND gnaw the furniture at the same time.

To combat your pup jumping up at kids, teach your dog that children only say, 'Hi' when your dog sits. But boy, oh boy, when the sitting happens, then the greetings and fuss are AMAZING!

So, there you go, in a nutshell – the principles for all of your dog training opportunities. To summarise:

- Strongly and energetically reinforce the behaviours you want more of.
- Set appropriate, achievable criteria.

🐾 Don't be too proud to lower criteria and only raise the bar when you're hitting 10 out of 10.

🐾 When you're both proficient in one environment, change the location of your practice sessions to ensure your exercises are robust.

🐾 For unwanted behaviours, use watertight Control and Management to prevent them happening.

🐾 Then heavily reinforce the alternative Mutually Exclusive Behaviour so everyone's happy.

And remember, always constantly review your training sessions and make them fun and enjoyable – both you and your dog should be delighted with each training opportunity.

Enjoy the process, it's not a race!

TOILET TRAINING

Ah, nothing illustrates how much we love our French Bulldog puppy as much as the commit-ment we show when toilet training! Imagine giving any other visitor to your house the benefit of the doubt when you spot a little 'mistake' on the carpet!

There are many things to consider regarding *why* dogs may toilet indoors: maybe they're just puppies and haven't yet learned the best place to wee and poop; maybe it's just physically impossible for such young dogs to 'hold on', because full bladder control may take up to 20 weeks to develop. (Yep! Twenty weeks, you are in it for the long haul.) Or maybe the indoor toileting isn't simply a case of

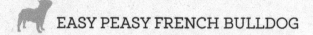

needing 'to go', but a symptom of pure excitement when visitors come to the house. (Be honest, we've all done it!)

For older dogs, inside toileting may be a symptom of stress, a urinary tract infection (UTI), digestion or dietary issues. If your French Bulldog is over 20 weeks old and toilet training isn't going as you would've hoped, then a call to the vet is definitely in order to make sure your dog is as comfortable and healthy as possible.

If you're now the proud forever-home-giver to a lucky rescue French Bulldog, then bear in mind that it may take a little while to get on top of the toilet training, as the new surroundings and upheaval in their life may not only cause a little stress, but the dog's previous surroundings may have dictated through necessity that toileting indoors is the norm.

So, medical issues aside, there are a few essential tools to ensure success when toilet training your French Bulldog:

- 🐾 A pee/poop diary
- 🐾 An enclosed area such as a puppy pen
- 🐾 A keen eye for canine body language
- 🐾 Commitment
- 🐾 Correct enzymatic cleaning products

SET UP FOR SUCCESS

As much as possible, until your French Bulldog is fully toilet trained, they shouldn't be left unattended in an area where they've *previously* left you an unwelcome pressie on the carpet, or in an area that you REALLY don't want them to soil. Of course, that doesn't mean that you must be with your dog 24/7 when indoors. It just means that someone is there to watch them in case they start showing predictive body language suggesting that they may need the toilet – such as sniffing the floor or turning slowly in a tight circle. If someone can't be with them, then pop them in an enclosed area such as their puppy den or kitchen area – ideally the place where they regularly eat and sleep. Dogs, like most animals, try to refrain from soiling the area where they eat and sleep. Most will also avoid toileting on hard surfaces if they can help it, so the kitchen area may be ideal.

In contrast to some traditional advice, I don't advise putting down newspaper or 'puppy pads' indoors for your dog to toilet on. In my opinion, this practice encourages the habit of toileting inside, which is the polar opposite of what we eventually want. Regular and appropriate periods outside as listed overleaf, combined with committing to observing or containing your dog when inside, will initially take more effort than just laying

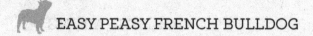

down newspapers and pads, but it will pay greater divid-ends in terms of teaching your dog correct toilet habits.

As with all unwanted behaviour (such as peeing indoors!), when we're utilising the potency of positive reinforcement, the most important thing is that we teach your French Bulldog the behaviour we DO want them to repeat in future, and with toilet training, that's very much 'doing your business outside'!

I want you to heavily reinforce the behaviour of toileting outside at *every* opportunity until the toilet training is mastered. As soon as your dog *finishes* going to the toilet outside, you're going to reinforce that behaviour with plenty of treats and affection. That is *how* you're going to reinforce toilet training outside.

The next question is *when* ... namely, when is the most opportune time to bring your dog outside to do the deed?

The times when your French Bulldog is most likely to want to go to the toilet – and therefore earn reinforcement – are:

- 🐾 First thing in the morning
- 🐾 After eating
- 🐾 After waking
- 🐾 After play
- 🐾 After a visitor arrives
- 🐾 After any excitement indoors

- 🐾 If you see your dog sniffing and circling the floor
- 🐾 Last thing at night

At any of these times, pick up or encourage your dog outside to the designated toileting area and, above all, be patient!

Don't use this time outside to immediately start playing or fussing with your dog. If you do so, the pair of you may take your mind off the reason you've actually gone outside. Plus, I'd much rather you keep the fun and games as part of the reinforcement process along with the treats. The clearer we can differentiate between the pre-wee and post-wee activities, the sooner your Frenchie will learn the lesson that 'toileting outside makes the good times START'.

So, once you have successfully spotted the body language and/or signs that your dog needs to toilet and you are outside with them, give your dog a good five to 10 minutes to sniff and wander while you remain passive. Poised, but passive!

If your dog doesn't toilet, no problem at all, just pop them back inside where you can watch them, or in their enclosed area where they feel happy but are unlikely to toilet.

After five minutes, 'rinse-and-repeat' by the pair of you going back outside to try again...

When your dog does go to the toilet outside, remember

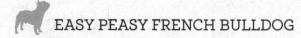

EASY PEASY FRENCH BULLDOG

to treat and praise generously *as soon as they finish*. A few treats and a great game are much cheaper than a new carpet!

Note, I said to treat and praise *as soon as your dog finishes their toileting.* That's so important ... simply because too many people get so excited when their dog starts to pee that they quite literally interrupt the flow to start the celebrations. The result being that the dog learns to half-pee outside, grabs the treat then runs back inside to dispense the remaining 50% of the goods. Oopsie!

It may seem a little belt-and-braces, but I'm a big fan of new French Bulldog owners keeping a pee/poop diary. (You can call it something else if you're going to keep it on your office desk!) The benefit of this diary is that after a few weeks, you'll start to see a pattern around the times your dog is most likely to go to the toilet. Armed with such advanced intelligence, you'll soon know the best times to bring them outside in order to give you and your puppy the best chance of success.

If your dog does have an accident and toilets inside – and this is REALLY important – _do not tell them off_. The last thing we want is your dog feeling anxious around you. Telling them off will damage your relationship and you may end up with unwanted lessons learned, such as your dog thinking it's not safe to toilet when you're around, inside or out!

So, if your dog has an accident indoors, accept that you need to be more vigilant in future and simply wash the area thoroughly with a good enzymatic cleaner. No biggy. It's just part of the process and toilet training is no different to any other kind of training: always a *process*, never an *event*.

Sometimes, being the friendliest dogs in the world, Frenchies can get so excited about meeting new people and visitors in the house that they can't help but pee a little as they say, 'Hello'. This 'greeting wee' or 'submissive wee' is not uncommon and, generally, as the dog's confidence grows with experience and maturity, the problem tends to rectify itself.

If you have an overly excitable greeter, simply make sure that visitors initially meet your dog outside and try to keep greetings pleasant and kind, but low-key, to limit any initial over-arousal. Long term, always seek to develop and expand your dog's confidence around people and new environments, not with arousal but with calm and loving reassurance.

It's really important, so I will reiterate – always avoid the temptation to tell off or punish your dog for making a mistake as this will only make them more frightened and submissive next time, which will exacerbate the problem and break down any trust.

If you've got a shy pup or taken on a rescue dog that may still be finding their feet, make sure you keep all greetings and

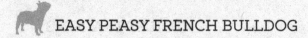

interactions with new visitors as gentle as possible. Rather than the visitor automatically yelling and leaning over your dog to exuberantly say, 'Hi', ask them to crouch down and encourage the dog to them, so your French Bulldog always feels they have choice and agency in the situation.

Toilet training is a wobbly bridge all owners need to cross, so don't be too hard on yourself and *never* be too hard on your dog. Keep your eyes on the prize and remember, if you give yourself every opportunity to reinforce the behaviours you want more of by keeping your diary, going outside at the most opportune times and making sure your supervision is on-point by using your enclosed areas, or watching your dog like a hawk for pre-wee tell-tale signs ... you'll both crack this challenge just as soon as your dog is able.

TRAINING: SIT

Chances are, Sit is going to be the most frequent behaviour you ask your dog to do. So, let's make sure we get it right from the start!

Performing a Sit will put your French Bulldog in the perfect position for you to pop their lead on and off or for a bit of safety when you are out and about. Perfecting the Sit is also going to be a great skill to help your Frenchie AVOID doing unwanted behaviours, such as jumping up on strangers in the park to say a hearty 'Hello', and is far more preferable to them clambering up the side of the ice-cream van as you're paying for your 99!

As a French Bulldog owner yourself, I don't need

to tell you this, but you won't have failed to notice why breed characteristic descriptions often use words such as 'exuberant' and 'outgoing', which are both tremendously beautiful and welcome traits, but it's vital that we *channel* those traits into behaviours that work well for everyone.

If our French Bulldogs want to say, 'Hello' to the visitor at the door, or they'd like a tasty treat thank-you-very-much, well, let's teach them that a polite bottom on the floor leads to all things good, as opposed to a jump-up-ambush-smash-and-grab life ethos!

Regardless of the age of your French Bulldog, let's start from the very beginning to build a great foundation for the Sit, then accelerate from there, so your visitors and ice creams continue to remain in one piece!

We're going to start by first luring the behaviour with a treat; after that, we'll move on to adding a cue to the behaviour, which means naming the behaviour 'Sit'; and then we're going to learn how to get the behaviour even at times when there's no treat in your hand.

Once we have the behaviour nice and reliable and 'on cue', we're going to raise the bar by adding the 3Ds, so more Duration, Distance and Distraction, to the training sessions. All of this will mean, that no matter what else is going on around us, Sit means Sit!

1. **Luring the Sit**

   Engage your Frenchie's nose by holding a treat for them to sniff as they (no doubt!) lurk in front of you.

   Slowly move the treat up above your dog's head and you'll notice that as they raise their head to follow your hand, the weight in their hips will rock back and down towards the floor. As their butt touches the floor, say, 'Good!' and pop the treat in their mouth.

   If they remain in the Sit position, fantastic, pop another treat into their mouth to illustrate that remaining in the Sit position pays well! If they move out of the Sit position as soon as they get the first treat, no biggy – we're going to be working on Duration a little later on, so they'll soon learn to add patience to their repertoire!

   Remember to be as consistent as possible with your body language and pace of movement in these early stages, and aim to get five successful repetitions in five different locations over the next five days; I know ... slave driver, eh?!

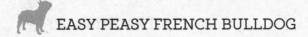

2. Adding the Cue

Now that you're getting a nice, fluent Sit with your luring, it's time to add a verbal *cue* so that when you say, 'Sit', your dog knows exactly what's required.

With a treat in your hand, again lure their head up as their nose follows the goodies, but this time, as they shift their weight backwards, just before their butt touches the floor say, 'Sit', and as soon as they complete the movement say, 'Good!' and pop a treat in their mouth for them to enjoy.

Repeat the above stage several times and, again, in several locations so the behaviour becomes super-reliable, no matter where you are.

3. Fading the Lure

Now that you've paired the word, 'Sit' prior to your French Bulldog going into the Sit position, it's time for us to start fading the treat as a lure to get the behaviour, so even if there's no food in your hand, you can be sure your dog will sit when you say, 'Sit'. I don't want you to become one of those moany dog owners who say, 'My dog only does it if there's a treat in my hand'. WE'RE BETTER THAN THAT, PEOPLE!

As before, lure with the treat in your hand

and say, 'Sit' to get a couple of swift successful repetitions so your Frenchie is in the groove and then, WITHOUT a treat in your hand, do the same consistent hand signal you've been doing all along ... say, 'Sit' and when your dog drops anchor, say, 'Good!' but this time, take the treat from your pouch and toss it a couple of metres away so your dog can go and get it – which means they'll naturally get out of the position and reset for the next Sit request.

Do several repetitions to reassure your dog that even though there's no treat in your hand when you give the verbal cue, they trust that the good times will come *after* they're achieved the behaviour you've asked for.

4. **Fading the Hand Signal**

This part is *simple*, but not necessarily easy, as it requires that rarest of commodities: <u>patience</u>!

It's fine to use a hand signal to get your 'Sit', but it's also important to train and prepare for times when maybe your dog can't see you, or perhaps you'll be in an unfamiliar body position with your hands already occupied, such as carrying a massive birthday cake with 50 lit candles on it – perhaps now

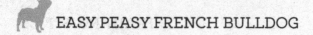

you can see why Sit is so much better than your dog jumping up willy-nilly!?

Here's the drill:

We're going to do these repetitions nice and fast to generate a bit of momentum. We all know how much Frenchies love to please, so I want your dog to almost be guessing what's coming next (clue: it'll be a 'Sit'!), and to offer the correct behaviour even though there'll be subtle body language changes following each successful repetition.

With just your full hand signal (remember, no treat in hand!), say, 'Sit' and, when your Frenchie completes their mission, say, 'Good!', then toss the treat for them to chase and enjoy.

As they enthusiastically return to you, again say, 'Sit', but only do a three-quarter version of your hand signal. When your dog pops their bottom on the floor say, 'Good' and toss a treat...

When they bound back to you excitedly, say, 'Sit' and do just 50% of your original hand signal. As soon as they sit, say, 'Good' and treat as before. You know what's coming next...

Next repetition, ask for a 'Sit' and give just a quarter of the original hand gesture and if successful, your final repetition will be...

... your French Bulldog expectantly running back to you

having just devoured their previously well-earned treat, and with you keeping your hands by your sides, you say, 'Sit' so your dog assumes the sitting position acting purely on your verbal cue. Success!

Treat, praise and play with your dog like they're the best thing in the world because, you know, they are!

If any of the above stages seem a little sticky at the moment, that's cool, just stay on that level for a while, build on success and don't move on to the next level until you're happy that what you're asking for is comfortably being achieved. Dog training should *never* feel like it's a race against time. Train the dog in front of you. Sometimes they'll be super-keen and other times they may need a little more encouragement and the *really* good treats to make sure their motivation and efforts are tip-top. If it's not happening, don't worry, bail out, have a cuddle and have a play. No pressure, tomorrow's another day. They're only human after all!

Once the pair of you are smashing it, it's time to attack the 3Ds again: Duration, Distance and Distraction.

Successfully getting your French Bulldog to Sit is great, but getting them to successfully Sit for you for extended periods of time, no matter how far away you are from each other and no matter what else is going on around you, is really next level stuff!

This is how YOU'RE going to achieve it!

For your Duration, Distance and Distraction sessions, I want you to practise sometimes with your hand signal, and sometimes with nice passive hands, so we can prepare for all eventualities.

DURATION

Ask your dog to Sit and, when they do, count one second in your head and if your dog has remained in their Sit, say, 'Good!' and toss a treat for them to scoff and then encourage them back to you for the next repetition.

Following each successful attempt, add another second to the next repetition, so if your previous attempt was a success at one second, make the next criteria two seconds. If that worked out well for you, go for three seconds, and so on.

Here's the deal: I need you to be honest at this point, because if one thing is inevitable, it's that your French Bulldog WILL move from the position before you say, 'Good' sooner or later. That's fine, that's dog training for you! Like I said earlier, I like to look at these repetitions not as failures but simply as feedback.

If your French Bulldog's Sit was solid at one second, solid at two seconds ... all the way up to seven seconds, but when you attempted eight seconds they got 'ants in their pants' and stood up before you got to say, 'Good', then what I want you to do is smile, say, 'Never mind, mate', keep hold of the treat this time, and on your next attempt consolidate and start again at one second, then hit success and reinforce your dog with their 'Good' and treat, which they so much deserve.

Next rep? Go for two seconds ...

Remember, dog training never goes in a straight line upwards and the most important thing is that you keep it fun, you keep it light, and you maintain enthusiasm and trust that the pair of you will get there together in the end.

Keep your sessions to around 10 repetitions to maintain novelty and enthusiasm, but if it so happens that your tenth attempt doesn't quite work out, drop down to one second and get a few successes before you call it a day – always try to end on a high and *always* end with a smile, a play and a cuddle. ALWAYS!

DISTANCE

Sometimes it is going to be really handy for you to not only pop your Frenchie into a Sit for a period of time, but also for you to have faith that your dog will remain safely in a Sit while you move some distance away, perhaps to help someone who's not particularly fond of dogs (weirdo!), or to go and pop the poop bag in the designated bin.

Ask your dog to Sit and, once they're settled, move just

one leg back a step (yours, not your dog's!), but leave the other leg in the remaining position. Count a second then return to your original position. If your dog has remained in a solid Sit, say, 'Good' and treat.

Next repetition: take one whole step away, return to your dog and treat as before.

Following each successful attempt, take an additional step away from your dog, wait a second or two, then return to reinforce.

Here's an additional little tip for you to ensure stability: when you return to your dog, wait a second or two, staying still, before you say, 'Good' and treat. This will help your dog avoid anticipating the 'Good' too early, resulting in the possibility of them breaking their position *as* you return, rather than the desired *once* you return.

As always, if you hit a tricky patch for your dog, lower the criteria back to one step, get success and increase distance a sliver at a time.

Aim for a success rate of at least nine out of 10. Less than nine and you're being too greedy, 10 out of 10 every time? C'mon, raise the bar!

DISTRACTION

My favourite criteria shift! This is when you get to act like an idiot, all in the name of *training*.

So far, you've got a nice solid Sit, you've taught your dog to maintain their Sit position for a good period of time AND your dog is able to remain in a Sit position, even if you need to walk a short distance away.

The final step is to really *ingrain* the behaviour by teaching your dog to be able to happily go into, and stay, in a Sit position for a period of time, no matter what other madness is going on around them!

This will really help in the real-world should you be surrounded one day by kids on bikes, or God help us, be stuck in the vet's reception on International 'Bring Your Cat to the Vet Day'!

Ask your dog to Sit, take one step away and tap your hand on your head three times before returning to reinforce your dog. (Note: this may seem simple but, do you know what, I bet your French Bulldog watches your hand like a hawk during training, especially as that's where the treats come from!)

As always with good dog training, to change something, you need to *change* something. If the movement is too much for your dog at this stage, try another repetition but move *muuuuch* slower, tap fewer times on your noggin or stay closer to your dog.

Remember, build success and train with honesty and integrity. Doing the same thing twice and expecting a different result is the definition of madness. Doing the same thing twice and expecting a different result is the definition of madness.

Following each successful repetition, add a steadily increasing catalogue of distractions, such as:

- 🐾 Hopping up and down on one leg

- 🐾 Whistling

- 🐾 Saying the alphabet

- 🐾 Tying your shoelace

- 🐾 Dropping a tennis ball and letting it bounce away

- 🐾 Spinning on the spot like Wonder Woman (send video to my socials for this one, please!)

Sit will definitely be one of the most common positions you ask your French Bulldog to do for you in a whole series of scenarios with a whole series of distractions throughout their life, so the peace of mind you'll have knowing that it's a strong, reliable behaviour will be worth its weight in gold.

TRAINING: RECALL

Unfortunately, too many people wait until they see their Frenchie's butt disappearing over the horizon in pursuit of several hundred pheasants before they say to themselves, *Oh, maybe I should think about teaching a Recall!*

I am going to teach you how to train your dog to come back to you with the use of a whistle. Don't worry, if you are not the whistling type, I'm also going to help you teach your dog to come back to the verbal cue of 'Come!'

To be fair, it doesn't matter whether you use a whistle or your voice to give the verbal cue 'Come'; in fact, you may well prefer to use a *verbal* Recall as you will always have your voice with you, but what does matter is <u>what the cue means to your dog</u>.

WE KNOW that to us the cue (whistle or verbal) for Recall means 'Run to me', but for your French Bulldog I want that Recall cue to mean that *great things are about to be produced from YOU, hence, they better leg it back to you ASAP!*

To start off with, we're going to use treats to *condition* the Recall cue. As French Bulldogs love to play with toys, we're going to progress to toys once we've taught your dog what the cue means. To begin with, however, the advantage to laying the foundations with food means we can do many, many repetitions in a short period of time, hence ingraining the potency of the cue nice and quickly. Here we go:

With plenty of tasty treats in your pouch and with your whistle on a lanyard around your neck, you're ready to get to work.

Head out with your dog into a quiet, familiar location such as your garden and just hang around for a while, let your dog have a sniff and a pee to become comfortable in the location, and to allow any initial novelty to the area dissipate before we start adding the cue. We don't want to have to compete with the environment, so if your Frenchie needs a little longer to become comfortable and to settle, no problem at all, take your time.

After a few minutes of silence have passed, and your dog is less animated, sneakily raise the whistle to your lips BUT, if your dog has spotted you placing the whistle in your mouth DON'T immediately blow it. I want your Recall cue to be the SOUND of the whistle, not the SIGHT of the whistle.

Get ready ... let a few seconds pass then *peep peep!*, blow two short pips of the whistle then immediately jog a couple of steps away from your dog and *when they come to you*, start to excitedly place individual treats into their mouth as you continue to step backwards.

After four to five treats, drop to one knee, give them a big fuss then STOP. Silently stand up and be as passive as you can...

This will seem a little odd to your dog, but I want the contrast between Recall and No-Recall to be as stark as possible. The clearer we can make the process, the easier it'll be for your dog to pair the 'peep peep' cue with the 'good times'.

The reason you're feeding your dog straight after the *peep peep* is (hopefully) obvious, but the reason I want you to step back as you treat is to keep the dog moving in towards you, always looking to reduce the distance between you and them as part of the Recall exercise.

Repeat this exercise two or three times, with the passive

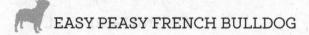# EASY PEASY FRENCH BULLDOG

periods of two to three minutes in between, then quit for that session. Don't do it to death in one session as we want to maintain the excitement, urgency and novelty of your Recall cue as much as we can at this early stage.

If you can find a few moments or a quiet spot on your dog walk, feel free to perform a little impromptu version of this exercise, because it will really advance your Recall training if you can build a strong foundation by practising in as many different locations as possible. You may want to keep your dog on a long line for safety reasons, which is fine, just make sure the line remains slack, we don't want the whistle to predict any pulling or discomfort, in fact, quite the opposite!

Once you can see a clear and happy head-flick towards you the second that you blow your whistle, we can add a little more animation to the proceedings and really start tapping into your Frenchie's hunting drive...

From a passive position, blow the whistle *peep peep* and jog backwards away from your dog. As soon as they start chasing towards you, and with you facing your dog, toss a treat further behind you in the direction they're running. Turn and face your dog again and as soon as they've eaten that treat and glanced up towards you, *peep peep*! Jog away again and throw another treat in the opposite direction, behind you again, for them to chase. As soon as they've grabbed that one from the ground, *peep peep* one last time as you drop to your knee, welcome them into you for a cuddle and the final treat (or two!).

Now you've started to condition not only the Recall, but also the *urgency*, we can introduce your dog's favourite toy.

Do exactly the same as above but when you *peep peep* your whistle, rather than producing the treats, jog away and produce the toy for your dog's favourite game of chase or ragging – whatever they most enjoy.

Remember, as your Recall training matures and develops, make sure you practise it in as many locations as possible. But don't push your luck too quickly, too soon.

If your dog is having a fantastic play with their other doggy mates and you're not prepared to bet £100 that they'd come if you blew your whistle, then guess what? Don't blow your whistle! Don't set up yourself or your dog for a fall.

If you think the level of distraction might be too high, then don't dilute the power of your cue by blowing the whistle only to be disappointed. In such scenarios, just go and get your dog, then figure out your training plan so you can build the stages of distraction up to the point where you're willing to bet that £100!

If you're walking in an area that may be too distracting, or indeed dangerous for your dog to be off-lead, then please just attach them to a five- or 10-metre-long line so you can stay in contact – ALWAYS keep your best friend safe.

If you've got a Frenchie that loves their food (show me one that doesn't!), then think of other scenarios where you can pair the *peep peep* with good times from you. Perhaps at mealtimes, let them out into the garden as you prepare their food bowl, then sneakily open the back door... *PEEP PEEP!* then place their bowl on the doorstep for them to enjoy.

Even if you plan to use a whistle for your outdoor Recalls, it's definitely worth going through all of the above stages with you using your voice and calling 'Come' instead of the whistle's *peep peep*, as in future you may need a more subtle way to call your dog, or perhaps your Recall training may start interfering with the referee's authority at the local football pitches!

TRAINING: LOOSE LEAD WALKING

Pretty much, you're going to want your dog to walk nicely on the lead every day for the rest of their life, so it's important that you invest a generous amount of training time in achieving that particular skill.

Loose Lead Walking is all about having a *connection* with your dog. That said, we don't need your dog to be constantly staring at you and trotting along like a competition show pony, because we want them to be able to sniff, look around and enjoy the environment as much as we do. However, if we can train your French Bulldog to check-in with you every now and then, and to stay within a certain perimeter of you when on-lead, then we're in business!

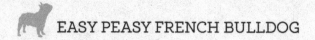

The equipment I'd like you to use is:

A *Lead*: approximately 1.5–2 metres in length. I want the lead to have a decent length, which in turn will give ample opportunity to work with a relaxed connection between the pair of you. Too often, owners make the mistake of trying to work with a short lead, which automatically becomes taut, prohibiting the opportunity to work with, and reinforce, Loose Lead Walking.

Treat Pouch: Timing of reinforcement is *key*, so rather than fumbling about in your pocket through piles of used tissues, your car keys and a couple of old mints in order to find a dog treat, get yourself a treat pouch that you can clip on to your belt for rapid reinforcement!

STATIONARY CONNECTION

Let's start to build connection slowly and stationary at first, then look to add movement and pace to create the Loose Lead walking dream...

In a nice, quiet and familiar location, pop your dog on the lead and stand still for a few moments. Quietly drop a treat on the floor for your dog to eat and, as soon as they do, quietly drop another, and another ... and another until you see your dog expectantly looking to the floor for the next goody.

Once you see evidence that your dog is anticipating the next drop, I want you to WAIT, don't make the drop, *wait*. You wait until your dog looks up to you – the source of the drops – as if to say, 'Hey, where's my next treat drop?' *As soon as they look up to you*, you say, 'Good!' to mark the behaviour of your dog looking to you, *then* drop the treat for them to enjoy, to reinforce the behaviour of your dog checking in with you.

Marking the behaviour with a 'Good' is your way of illustrating to your dog that whatever behaviour they did when you said, 'Good', is the behaviour that earned them the treat.

The better your timing is with your 'Good!', ie. *saying it the split-second the behaviour occurs*, the better your training will be, as your dog will soon learn what behaviour to offer again ... and again ... and again to get the much-appreciated reinforcement.

At this early stage, the reinforcement is a treat. Treats are great to use and, let's face it, DOGS LOVE TREATS! More importantly, it makes training more efficient as we can do rep after rep after rep. The more positive repetitions we can do in the early stages of training, the more effective our progress will be.

As your Loose Lead Walking develops, alternative reinforcers for checking in could be:

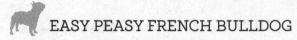

- Being let off the lead to go play.
- Crossing the road to continue their walk.
- Going out of the front door for their dog walk.
- A throw of the ball to chase (take them off-lead first unless you don't value your collar bone!).

Once you can pop your dog on the lead, stand stationary and your dog is looking to you to start the good times, we can then add a little movement into proceedings in order to start to develop the exercise into something that looks a little more like Loose Lead Walking.

So, once you are at this stage, when your French Bulldog looks up to you, say, 'Good', but this time start walking slowly with tiny steps as you pop the treat into your dog's mouth, rather than the previous methods of dropping the treat. Keep moving slowly as you hold the lead by the handle next to your belt buckle area with both your hands and the lead at full length. The reason I want both hands together by your belt buckle area is that this will help you resist the urge to pull back or inadvertently reach down to hold the lead at a shorter length, which would be counterproductive for what we want here!

As you slowly take a few steps to your left, then to your right, five or six steps forwards then a little backward walking to keep things interesting, I want you to say, 'Good' and treat your dog every time they glance up towards you. If you can, treat on the move; too often, owners only reinforce their dog in a stationary position. The fallout from never treating on the move is that the dog ends up thinking that it's only worth looking to the owner when stationary ... well, not on our watch!

Keep your movements to only five or six steps in any one direction at first, to prevent your dog from assuming where you're heading to, which may result in them forging ahead.

As a French Bulldog, full of exuberance and appetite, a problem you may initially encounter is your dog jumping up at you for the treats. Don't worry, you will easily combat that issue by ensuring you only say, 'Good!' and treat when your dog is walking nicely with all four feet on the floor. The timing of your 'Good!' is so important here: if you mistakenly say, 'Good' when your dog actually jumps up, don't worry, but seriously ... don't make a habit of it!

As you progress, you can increase your criteria by reinforcing every five steps of Loose Lead Walking, then every 10 steps, then every 20 and so on...

Practise in a nice, low-distraction location at first, but as you improve, you can mature on to higher-distraction environments such as town centres or the local park.

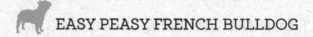

As always, be realistic! If a particular environment is too distracting at the moment for your dog to comfortably check in with you, adjust your expectations, rehearse in a lower-distraction environment for a while and, when you're ready, up the ante.

Here's the secret of dog training in a nutshell for you: find out what activity your Frenchie loves doing, then exchange *that* activity for the behaviour *you* want more of. Think of it like an equation: Loose Lead Walking = 'Find it!'

Your training walks can now start looking like this...

Walk with your dog by your side, quietly drop your dog's favourite toy as the pair of you keep walking forward, away from the dropped toy... when you're walking together, as soon as your dog glances up to you, say, 'Find it!' and turn with your dog to encourage them to rush back, have a good search culminating in a big celebration and exciting play as they rejoice in having found the toy for you!

Next rep: drop the toy, keep walking forward, but the criteria is now for your dog to check in with you for two steps before, 'Find it!'

Perhaps the next repetition will have a criteria of four steps on Eye Contact, or 10 steps of Loose Lead, you decide – the world's your oyster...

Exercises like this will not only keep walks interesting, but they will also keep the pair of you engaged with each other and will naturally improve your Loose Lead Walking and checking-in, so the pair of you can safely and comfortably enjoy future adventures together.

Remember, always put your dog in a position where they can be successful, reinforce well and appreciate that tomorrow's another day.

Loose Lead Walking is literally all about taking it one step at a time.

THE FRENCHIE GAME!

Fun times with your Frenchie are not only a source of pleasure for both of you, but will also increase the bond the pair of you have with each other. Plus, if we're clever, it will help you tap into those breed specific traits that make the French Bulldog so unique.

If I was a Frenchie, do you know the type of game I'd like to play with you? One that really gives me an opportunity to exercise and show off my hunting, chasing, grabbing and shaking skills – that'd be the game for me! So, let's give the Frenchie Game a go...

Take a tea towel and rip it into six strips. Tie a knot in each strip to give it a little extra weight and pop five of

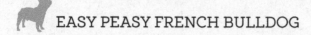

the 'Ratties' in your back pocket. (The strips may *look* like knotted tea towel bits to you, but for your Frenchie – they're now RATTIES!)

Take the remaining Rattie gently in your hand and, with your Frenchie watching (I admit this'll feel a little weird), quietly whisper and stroke the Rattie to ignite your dog's alertness and curiosity. I promise you, there's not a French Bulldog in the world that won't become super-nosey when Rattie is getting all the attention!

With Rattie enclosed in your cupped hands, slowly kneel down on the floor and place your hand over Rattie so your dog can't grab at it...

As your dog watches your hands over the trapped 'rat', wait until they're nice and still, showing a little self-control and patiently waiting for the 'rat' to escape...

Slowly say, 'Ready' ... 'steady' ... then ... 'GO!', as you flick the Rattie along the floor for your Frenchie to do what they do best – Chase! Grab! Shake!

As your dog shakes the living daylights from the tea towel strip, you can quietly get the next Rattie from your back pocket and when the shaking stops, gently call your dog back over to you to let them know you've yet ANOTHER rat in the trap, ready to escape...

Now, a 'live' Rattie ready to run is always more interesting than the shaken, now 'dead' rat in your dog's mouth, so as they spit out the deceased quarry and focus in on you again, you can begin to gently and quietly wind up the escape again with a 'Ready ... Steady ... Go!' and again flick the Rattie for carnage round two!

Once you've built up a bit of a rhythm, you'll begin to see the added benefits of this exercise. It started out as, and *remains*, a FUN activity – but, guess what, you'll get fantastic FOCUS on you when you say, 'Ready ... Steady...' And so, your Frenchie will learn the benefit of patience and SELF-CONTROL as they wait, poised for the Rattie to escape, and they'll learn to RECALL to you after a successful *hunt*, ready for the next escapee!

As with all good dog training, you'll be celebrating and expanding on your dog's natural abilities, rather than trying to suppress their innate drives. Not only that, the pair of you will be playing a new game – giving each other undivided attention and associating the good times with each other. Not a bad deal for the price of second-hand tea towel!

One final thought: to keep your dog happy and on an even keel, in addition to the activity listed above, never underestimate your own wonderful value to your dog.

Physical activities are lovely to enjoy with your dog, but with all of that ticked off, you can't beat simply sitting on

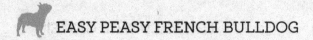

the grass with your Frenchie, watching the world go by with perhaps a smooth belly rub or a gentle ear scratch for good measure.

Time with your French Bulldog is very precious – spend it wisely.

COMMON FRENCH BULLDOG PROBLEMS

WHY DOES MY FRENCH BULLDOG CHEW?

Dogs of all ages are hard-wired to feel good when they chew – it's a natural and essential part of their day.

A puppy's urge to chew (seemingly everything!) is nature's way to help accelerate how they learn about the world around them. For instance, what's edible and what's not, what squeaks and what doesn't – 'Is this a rat? Is it something else?' Chewing for puppies also goes a huge way towards offering much-needed pain relief from teething, as well as persuading those puppy teeth to leave the jaw to make room for the adult dog teeth trying to push their way up through the gums.

Puppy teeth start to break through at approximately two to three weeks of age, during the 'Transitional Stage' of development. At this age, a puppy is now beginning to learn to play, investigating the world and even learning to find out what's 'alive or not', and consequently they need those razor-sharp teeth to aid their fact-finding missions.

At this age, puppies don't have much strength in their jaw, so the teeth need to be super-sharp to get the desired responses and information from the world. As a puppy heads towards 12 weeks of age and the jaw becomes stronger, then those 28 baby teeth begin to be pushed out by the set of 42 adult teeth that are impatiently waiting behind. Eighteen weeks is the time to start wearing slippers around the house because when you tread on one of those discarded puppy teeth, man, you're gonna know about it!

During this stage, it's important that you offer a wide variety of textures for your pup to chew: some days they'll need something soft or textured to offer relief, the next day they'll need something tougher with more resistance.

I tell the owners I work with, 'Your puppy has four hours'

worth of chewing per day, what would you rather they chew? You, the furniture or an appropriate toy?!' The trick isn't to try and stop them chewing; the trick is to appreciate they *have* to chew – it's natural and necessary. Therefore, the challenge for the owner is to *divert* that puppy chewing onto the right target to keep both owner and puppy happy and relaxed for many hours, or to not bother and suffer the consequences!

The world is full of potential puppy chews as far as your French Bulldog is concerned. The task of the owner is to make the appropriate chewing targets such as dog toys and/ or snacks attractive and accessible, and conversely to make the inappropriate targets, such as furniture legs and rugs, inaccessible unless the puppy is supervised to avoid any mistakes.

Exploration

Another motivator for puppies to chew is exploration. All babies need to explore as much and as soon as possible, to become familiar with the big wide world. Us human babies reach out and try to touch everything we can with our hands. Dogs aren't blessed with such limbs, so it's the puppy's mouth and teeth that need to knuckle down and explore everything. And I mean *everything*! Again, here's where you need to offer an ever-available variety of chews, or you'll be sorry!

Puppy Chews

Build up a good store and variety of chews. A good chew can help dogs relax as well as offering a mutually beneficial alternative to the furniture! Remember, different textures and resistance are important – in my opinion, food-chews should ideally be natural, so avoid those packed with preservatives. Also, natural alternatives will hopefully be long-lasting so you get plenty of bang for your buck. There are also options at home, too – you may find a humble carrot or sliced cucumber will be just the trick. For non-food chews, a variety of textures offered by rope toys, knotted tea towels or rubber bones may offer much-needed relief from teething or boredom.

Q: *When does a chew toy stop being a chew toy?*
A: *When your puppy finds something better to chew!*

Although younger dogs tend to be the main culprit, it's not all about puppies; older Frenchies also need lots of appropriate chewing opportunities throughout the whole of their lives, as even at a later age, chewing just intrinsically feels good. Older dogs are programmed to enjoy chewing in order to keep their jaws exercised, their teeth and gums healthy, and as a way to chill out and relax of an evening. Also, bear in mind that as dogs reach old age, it's tougher for them to find pleasure running and chasing as they used to do, in which case what better treat to offer the older, gentler dog than a great chew toy or long-lasting treat as they lay by your feet, knowing that you're always there for them?

WHY DOES MY FRENCH BULLDOG CHASE ... JOGGERS, CARS, BIKES, CATS ...?

All of our dogs are *pre-wired* from back in the day, when dogs roaming free had to provide supper for themselves. Part of the internal wiring that dogs have is called the Predatory Motor Pattern, which fuels and triggers the dog's motivation to sniff out, visually focus on, sneakily creep up on, chase, grab, bite, kill and eat their prey.

Of course, over the years, we've selectively bred and emphasised particular aspects of the Predatory Motor Pattern within particular individual breeds, to give us unique working abilities dependent on our choice of breed. A French Bulldog will generally adore the opportunity to really grab, bite and shake their prize. If these opportunities are not 'presented', your dog may well go looking for such opportunities themselves! The call to hunt can be strong.

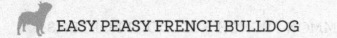

Depending on the individual dog, some aspects of this hunting pattern will be nearer the surface than others, but as anyone that has ever lived with a dog, or even just watched dogs in cartoons, knows, dogs love to chase!

As with all behaviours that dogs are hard-wired to enjoy doing, it's important that we don't look to suppress them, but to redirect these behaviours into more appropriate activities, as opposed to our dogs going self-employed! I like to imagine that a dog's internal drive is like an inflated, long balloon – you know the type of balloon I mean, the one that's always used as the body of the balloon modeller's sausage dog! If the air in the balloon is the dog's drive to chase and grab, as is the urge in many French Bulldogs, we may well try to *suppress* that drive by squeezing the balloon, but that will only result in the balloon expanding even more elsewhere, resulting in the pressure to escape getting greater and greater until ... BANG!

The trouble is, the dog doesn't need to successfully catch the target (jogger, car, bike, cat...) to get their reward; simply the opportunity and action of the chase feels so damn good inside that the chase behaviour itself is reward enough.

Our plan of attack here is two-fold: firstly, we need to ensure we have good Control and Management to prevent the dog from practising the unwanted behaviour; secondly, we need to provide a constructive outlet so the dog can get their 'chase' on, without causing havoc at the local park-run or kiddies' bicycle race!

Control and Management to Help With a Dog That Chases

If your dog is likely to want to chase anything they shouldn't, then while in training, try to avoid areas where the temptation may be at best frustrating, and at worst disastrous. That doesn't mean limiting or reducing the exercise your dog gets, it simply means early morning walks in the park may be better than busy lunchtimes, or perhaps a quiet local village green may be better than the local playing fields near the school. In addition, ensure that your lead and harness are in good repair, so you always have a safe contact and control of your dog.

Suitable Outlets

As a young dog training apprentice, I was always taught that 'If it's *in* the dog, it'll come *out* of the dog'. That means that if the dog has a high drive to chase or grab, then it's not a matter of *if*, but *when*.

So, how can we constructively satisfy our dog's drive to chase and grab, maybe even turn it to our advantage by swimming with the tide rather than fighting against it? Simple: play!

If you know your dog loves to chase, make sure that YOU'RE the source of such joy.

Think about how you play. Rather than holding the toy in your hands and encouraging them to instantly grab, try tying the toy to a metre-length of string or an old lead, and build up a little curiosity in your dog by whispering and 'stroking' the toy gently in your cupped hands, then entice your dog by dropping the toy to the ground then tweaking the 'prey' along the ground with the string. Once they start stalking or chasing the toy, flick it back up into your hands to maintain the novelty and to ensure there's more urgency from your dog the next time the 'prey' tries to 'escape' along the ground!

Drop the toy again and if there's interest, speed up the movement and verbally praise your dog as they chase and ultimately catch the fleeing toy. ONCE it's in their mouth, you can have a good old raggy game with them. When you're ready to start playing, you can simply swap the toy for a treat.

Once the pair of you are in the zone and you've got fantastic focus from your dog onto you – as you're now 'the warren' that the 'rabbit' runs from – you can untie the string and throw the toy for your dog to chase. As chase is the ultimate in canine capers, they'll be looking to return the toy to you, so you can launch it a second, third and fourth time, and give them the opportunity to show off their amazing chasing skills.

If your dog isn't so keen to return with the thrown toy once they've captured it, simply take a second identical toy from your pocket as soon as the first toy is in the dog's mouth. Believe me, the animated toy that you become interested in will be FAR more attractive than the 'dead' toy in your dog's mouth. You can't chase a 'dead' toy!

Regarding the toys that you use, make sure they're made from a material that's comfortable for your dog to grab, a suitable size for your pocket (and their mouth!) and, if you're working with a dog that can cover plenty of mileage, make sure the toy has a bit of weight so you can really launch it!

Once you've built up a love of the chase game, you can start to use it not only as an outlet for your dog's needs, but also as a reinforcement tool for your training.

Give the start of the chase game a name such as 'HERE!'. Stand quietly with the toy hidden, shout 'HERE!', then instantly pull out the toy and have the game of all games.

Once you've performed this routine over several days in several places, you now have your emergency Recall cue of 'HERE!' should you ever misjudge your dog walking location (which you won't!), or your dog goes bananas the second a skateboarding cat passes you by (which they could!).

Above all else, when out and about with your dog,

prevention is always better than cure. Spend your walks TOGETHER. Don't wander off in different directions either physically or in focus. That's when 'things on the horizon' begin to get enticing and an unwanted chase might begin. Play games together and reinforce any kind of checking-in with you with treats and praise.

If your dog is getting their needs accommodated by you, including their real doggy needs such as the drive to chase and grab, then there'll be no need for them to go thrill-seeking elsewhere!

WHY DOES MY DOG DIG?

Dogs dig!

Some dig a little in a very acceptable way, for example simply plumping up their bedding to make it more comfy; some dogs, however, dig A LOT!

There are many reasons a dog likes to dig: fluffing up their bed; digging a hole in the garden to lie in so that heavy-coated dogs such as Malamutes or Huskies can cool down; searching for tasty fibrous roots to chew; trying to track down the creature that's sending enticing scratching sounds or scrummy creepy crawly odours to the surface of the garden; digging up the treat, bone or chew that they *might* have buried there last week! And maybe a good old dig of the garden is simply just a fun, physical workout. Who are we to judge? ... We run on stationary treadmills!

As part of the dog's waste-not-want-not attitude to food, sometimes dogs will not be able to finish all of their food – maybe they're full, they're unable to chew through the tough material in one sitting or they don't feel quite safe to chow-down – so they'll look to dig and bury their food for a later date. They're creating a *cache*.

You'll notice that they'll dig with their feet, but will replace the soil with their nose. My little Chihuahua, Nancy, does this when she steals a tougher chew off one of my larger dogs! If your dog's an inappropriate digger, here's your plan of attack...

Make sure there's nothing stressing your dog that's causing them to look for sanctuary below ground by digging. For example, fireworks outside the house may often cause a dog to 'dig' the carpet. When scared, dogs look to go low, whereas cats look to go high. In firework season, you may need to build a snug den for your dog with plenty of heavy blankets over a crate (for your cat, simply clear a bookshelf!).

For indoor diggers, make sure you've no leaky pipes under your flooring. You'd be surprised how much water from a

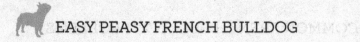

copper pipe sounds to your dog like a call-out from a lairy mouse!

If you've a precious area of your garden that you want to *keep* precious, temporarily fence that area off from your dog, or accompany your French Bulldog when in the garden to avoid unwanted rotavation. If you can't be with them in the garden, give them something better to do, such as a stuffed food toy to keep them occupied.

Finally, as idle paws do the devil's work, make sure your dog is getting plenty of physical exercise and mental outlets, and what better way than to create a special digging area that they ARE allowed to use – one that's a safe distance away from the newly planted bulbs! You don't need a large area, just one with loose, fresh soil or a mixture with sand, that you can hide a few pieces of treasure in, such as chews or toys. For the first few visits, go out with your dog and enjoy the dig together, make sure you celebrate each find and see the activity at first as a team game. After a few repetitions, I'm sure your dog will be able to somehow manage without you!

WHY DOES MY DOG DO...
THE ZOOMIES?!

'The Zoomies? What are "the Zoomies?"' I hear you say.

Well, everything has posher names nowadays, so some clever clogs in swanky meeting rooms refer to the Zoomies as FRAPS, or Frenetic Random Activity Periods, to be precise, madam!

Either way, the Zoomies is when your dog, for no *obvious* reason and usually in the evening, runs around the house like a lunatic as if their tail is on fire or they've just found the last Willy Wonka golden ticket and they don't know where to hide it!

The Zoomies run can look quite spectacular if not a little disconcerting: the dog runs super-fast in wide circles, sometimes with sudden stops or changes of direction and, as you may well know, dramatic leaps on to settees or spectacular crashes into human legs are not unheard of.

Although the exact motivation behind Zoomies is a little unclear, the purpose is to relieve stress and arousal, plus an outlet to blow off excess energy. Both reasons are understandable and, in my experience, there's a fairly common pattern. Zoomies normally happen with younger dogs, which makes sense as they're generally fed a high-quality food that gives them plenty of energy, but are perhaps limited in their physical and mental release opportunities due to their age and vaccination status.

Zoomies commonly occur in the evening and, again, this makes perfect sense. Dogs are *crepuscular* (I know, great word, eh?), which means they're programmed to become most active at twilight, aka, HUNTING TIME!

The trick is to know your dog and the common denominators in play when your Frenchie last had the Zoomies – observe these because they are likely to be the same triggers for a Zoomies session in the future. Triggers to look out for are pre- or post-feeding time, bath-time, exciting visitors or family members at the front door and, of course, walkies time!

Here's the good news: Zoomies are just *normal dog behaviour*. In fact, it's normal for lots of other species too, including horses, ferrets, cats and – clear the coffee table for this one – elephants!

Young dogs normally grow out of the Zoomies although one of my dogs, a seven-year-old whippet called Spider, still has the odd, very odd burst of the Zoomies – particularly if he has just found his favourite chew which he buried in my slipper yesterday or when 'Dad's home!'

Trying to stop the Zoomies can at best be a thankless task and, at worst, cause conflict and frustration, so I find the best remedy is to see out the 60 seconds or so of the storm, or in Spider's case, throw a toy to redirect the dog's pent-up energy onto some poor unsuspecting teddy bear!

Zoomies: live with them, enjoy them. Believe me, you'll miss them when they're gone!

So, we've nailed the chewing, the digging and the zooming – what's next?!

WHY DOES MY DOG JUMP UP ?

Don't panic!

Jumping up is a normal behaviour in dogs of all ages ... until, of course, you teach them an even more profitable behaviour!

Young dogs will naturally target their focus on Mum's face to lick the commissure (a posh term for 'corners') of her mouth, which in turn stimulates her to regurgitate food which the puppy then eats. Yum. It's therefore a natural progression for a dog to jump up at humans who are their new family in search of further attention and reinforcement (i.e. supper!).

The issue with dogs jumping up at humans is that not everyone appreciates dirty paw prints all over their new outfit, some people may be frightened by a dog jumping up at them and some children or older folk with sensitive skin may be inadvertently hurt by a dog's claws or – because your Frenchie simply ADORES PEOPLE – potentially knocked over altogether.

Okay, so how to improve the behaviour of a serial jumper-upper? As always, our first job here is to manage the environment so the dog doesn't get inadvertently reinforced for the undesired behaviour, and to heavily reinforce a new, *alternative* behaviour.

This is where we tap into what you learnt about 'Mutually Exclusive Behaviour' on pages 52–53. If you recall, the idea is simple: if your dog is doing a Mutually Exclusive Behaviour, then they cannot be doing the unwanted behaviour at the same time. Specifically for this section, if your French Bulldog is sitting, then they cannot be jumping up at the same time! Sounds simple, eh?!

The trick here (and everywhere else in your/their training career!) is to teach your dog what behaviour <u>works best</u> for them.

In the case of over-exuberant greetings that lead to jumping up, the goal for your French Bulldog is to say, 'Hello!' First things first, what behaviour do we

NOT want to reinforce by saying 'Hello'? Obviously ... jumping up.

What alternative behaviour would we prefer to reinforce? A cracking, bum-on-floor Sit is a great Mutually Exclusive Behaviour to combat jumping up. Sit tends to be a behaviour that gets practised a lot, so let's use it to everyone's advantage, including your dog's, to ensure everyone gets what they want. Time to get on with the training.

To start off, set up greeting opportunities in 'low-arousal' areas such as the back garden, and once you and your dog begin to nail your training, you can promote yourselves to more arousing environments such as the front door, which tends to be a real hot-spot for jumping up as that's where all the exciting visitors tend to arrive, but don't forget to proof your training by practising in as many locations as possible.

Step 1: Practise Sits in as many different places as possible to really embed the behaviour. Once you're happy that your dog's Sit is super-robust and they are responding with enthusiasm each time on the very first cue, then we can start adding other humans into the mix.

Step 2: Have your dog on the lead, ask your helper to approach slowly and to stop two metres away. Then ask your dog to 'Sit' and, when they do, give your dog a treat. Then, the most precious two words your dog can hear, give the cue, 'Say Hello' and have your helper crouch down to meet the dog at their own level – this will eliminate the desire for your dog to jump up.

This routine means you get what you want – the absence of jumping-up – and in exchange your dog gets what they want – a treat from you AND the much-coveted greeting!

Step 3: As you progress with success, raise the bar a little by having the helper come in a little faster, a little closer or a little more animated. Extra points for silly walks!

As long as your dog continues to Sit when cued, you can then progress to the previous scenes-of-the-crime, such as the front door or school gates.

Now, here's an additional twist...

Although most people don't want their dog to jump up onto people, some folk, maybe you included, DO enjoy your dog launching at you from 30 yards like a hairy missile to cover you in love and slobber! That's cool by me, all I want you to do is to verbally CUE the behaviour, so your dog knows when it IS okay for them to jump up ... and when it isn't.

To do this, sit in a chair to make this first stage easier then, with a treat, entice your dog's front feet up onto your shins or knees, depending on (A) the size of your dog and (B) the length of your legs! As your dog's feet make contact with you, say 'Cuddles' and pop the treat into their mouth. (If someone's watching, you may want to say something more macho than 'Cuddles'!)

Once your dog is comfortably hopping onto you while you're in the sitting position, you can progress to you being stood upright. Now you have a choice: Sits for polite greetings or if you ever want it, 'Cuddles' when you want to get a little more passionate with your *bonjours!*

TEACHING YOUR FRENCH BULLDOG TO BE HAPPY 'HOME ALONE'

There's nothing less exciting than the phrase 'prevention is better than cure', but believe me, a pinch of prevention now can save you and your dog A LOT of stress further down the line!

We all know the amazing character traits a French Bulldog arrives with, and that's why we adore them. However, sometimes their love of being with us and the intense desire they have to bond and be our best friend can work against them, resulting in stress (for all parties) when we're apart.

However, if we're not careful, some dogs may suffer when left alone. There can be all sorts of reasons for this. Perhaps the next-door neighbour decided to trial their new drum kit the last time you went out. Some dogs may simply get bored twiddling their thumbs when left in solitary confinement and this will often mean they get up to mischief. And, worrying as it is, some dogs may just descend into a pure panic when separated from someone they love.

I'm planning on helping you to build positive associations for your Frenchie when they are left alone, so we never get in a position of your dog being stressed at home. To aid you with this very important task, it is helpful to familiarise yourself with signs that your dog might display indicating they're already stressed at the prospect of being left alone, or that they struggled when you last went out:

- Pacing, whining, following you like a shadow or being hyper-vigilant as you prepare to go out.

- If you see evidence of unwanted ripping, scratching or chewing that's happened while you were absent, especially in the areas of your exit, these are signs that your dog has desperately tried to get to you.

- House soiling or an inability to eat any treats or chews that you left for your dog (a result of stress).

- Barking, howling or other vocalisation. Your neighbour will soon let you know, no doubt! Barking as a symptom of separation anxiety is usually done intermittently, as a 'call-and-response' pattern. The dog usually barks barks

barks, then waits for a few moments in silence to listen out for a 'reply' from their loved ones.

To complement and balance that selectively bred urge for your dog to be with you, it's important that as soon as possible we teach our dogs that not only is it okay to be alone for periods of time, it can actually be pretty cool!

Let's start by building a positive association to their 'safe area'. The safe area is the place you're going to be leaving your dog in when you go out for periods of time. Make sure the area is (obviously) safe, but also nice and comfortable and not somewhere that's going to be easily disturbed by noises outside, such as your drumming neighbour or a fox in the garden with a trombone...

At this stage, we're not yet looking to leave your dog, we're simply showing your French Bulldog that the safe area is a great place to be, where only good things occur.

Depending on the age of your dog and the layout of your house, the safe area needs to be a place where your dog will have plenty of room to comfortably choose to lay down, be able to locate and enjoy treats, but also an area where you can progress to being able to happily leave them, especially for our early stages of isolation.

Let's imagine the safe area is going to be your kitchen. Pop a child gate across the kitchen door opening (this

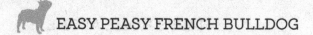

will help with our Distance and Duration exercises later on).

Before you even let your Frenchie into the area, I want you to scatter a few of their favourite treats, maybe leave a tasty chew in there for them to discover, and have their favourite, most comfortable bed in there for them to retire to, when the time comes.

With a sense of happy ceremony, open the child gate and allow your dog to enter the kitchen to discover and enjoy the treasure within. I want you to enter the room with your dog so they can focus 100% on the good vibes, without worrying that you may abandon them, but when you're in there, just stay nice and passive. The reason I don't want you too involved is that I want the positive associations made to the *area*, more so than with you – no offence!

After a few minutes, remove your dog from the area. Don't worry that they haven't yet finished all of their treats or got round to enjoying the food you stuffed into the toy for them. I WANT them to have in the back of their mind, *I can't wait to get back into that area again!* It's this conditioning and optimistic attitude to the future which is going to help create our Happy-Home-Alone-Frenchie.

After several repetitions over several days, start extending the time your dog is in the area, and when they get round to it, encourage them to enjoy their favourite chew or food-stuffed toy on their comfortable bed.

Over time, as your dog relaxes in the area, start to increase the distance between you and your dog: the other side of the kitchen at first; then, as long as your dog shows no signs of stress and maintains a nice display of relaxed body language, start going to the other side of the child gate, with you still remaining in view so there's no need for your dog to panic, or if you're lucky, not even look up from their tasty treats!

As I say, the plan here is to take our time and over a series of weeks take lots of tiny little steps in the right direction rather than being too pushy and 'poisoning' the safe area or set-up by causing your dog to panic or become suspicious as a result of you trying to run before you can walk.

In nice, small, incremental steps, you're going to be popping to the other side of the gate, in view for a few seconds before returning to your dog; then leaving the kitchen, closing the gate, counting a few seconds then returning; then ultimately leaving your dog happily in the kitchen, closing the gate and disappearing out of sight but remaining in the house for a minute or two, before returning to your dog and going about your business as normal.

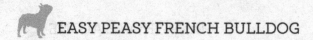

Note: when returning to your dog, don't make a big deal out of the return, no big fanfare or 'Where have you been all of my life?' embraces – this'll only add unwanted arousal to the situation and make your future absences even more stark.

As the duration of your absences increases, don't feel the need to add more and more treats to the area in order to 'keep your dog busy'. The training here isn't to *distract* your dog during your absence; it's purely to build a positive association to the situation where they *know* you're away, but they're learning that the situation can have a positive association, that you always return, and that they're learning to comfortably cope.

Also, as the duration of your absences increases, you can also add distance and work through potential hotspots such as opening and closing the front door or starting your car engine if it's within your dog's hearing distance. Be aware that these particular triggers may be especially sensitive for your dog, so during training, make sure you return to your dog nice and promptly after the trigger to ensure an absence of concern.

EQUIPMENT

My suggested equipment list will help you give 'home-alone' time a positive spin:

- ❧ Child gate: to set a clear perimeter of the safe area and to assist in building distance.

- ❧ Treats: lots of! Used to scatter within the safe area for your dog to discover.

- ❧ Snuffle mat: a kind of a 1970s bathroom shagpile mat used to hide treats within and to encourage, well, snuffling!

- ❧ Rubber toy: stuffed with food. Helps build duration, and chewing can be a relaxing and stress-releasing activity for your dog.

- ❧ Chews: safe, healthy and long-lasting please!

- ❧ Smart phone or camera: so you can keep a sneaky eye on your dog to make sure they're not getting frantic in your absence.

SUPPORTING EXERCISES

I cover Sit training extensively in this book, so use this exercise and concentrate on the Distance and Duration elements so your dog can feel good about you moving away from them. Use the same principles for teaching a Down on their favourite bedding.

Ensure your Frenchie is getting plenty of healthy physical exercises on a daily basis, so boredom is never a reason for getting into mischief!

BODY LANGUAGE

Throughout all of your training, ensure that your French Bulldog displays a nice happy body language. We like to see a relaxed spine, soft, happy facial expression with an open mouth and soft eyes – this indicates that your dog feels safe, happy and optimistic. If this is the kind of body language your dog is displaying during home-alone training, you're on the right track and, you know what, you can probably move on to the next level of Distance or Duration. Go you!

If, at any stage of the training, your dog displays hard, staring eyes, tail tucked or tension throughout their spine or hips – SLOW DOWN. Go back a step or two to rebuild optimism and to make sure you don't ruin the effort that you've already put in.

As a young trainer, I was always taught, 'The fastest way to train is slowly.' Tiny steps in the right direction ... that's the key. In my experience, the owners that achieve the greatest success in home-alone training are the owners that do LOTS of reps, and those that raise criteria SLOWLY.

Hopefully you can start from the beginning, build a positive association and never have to deal with the fallout out of isolation issues. However, if your dog already has a negative association with being home-alone, do the training as described, but if you do need to leave your Frenchie for a period of time that you haven't yet built up to in training, recruit the services of your family, friends, a trusted dog walker or day-care facility to make sure your dog isn't pushed beyond their isolation limits before they're ready.

Build trust, build predictability, build confidence, avoid suspicion and – as always – make sure you BOTH enjoy the process.

GROOMING YOUR FRENCH BULLDOG

The French Bulldog has a short-haired, fine, silky coat which is easy to manage at home. Frequent grooming will help form a bond between you and your dog, then it can become a lifelong shared experience that will be enjoyable and relaxing for both of you. From a health point of view, obviously we are looking to remove clumps, thorns or other items from the coat, but it's also worth noting that regular grooming helps to remove dead skin, brings out the natural oils of your dog's coat and stimulates circulation of blood to the skin, which all helps give a sleek and glossy condition.

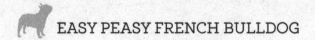

The tools you will need are:

- 🐾 Grooming mitt
- 🐾 Universal slicker brush
- 🐾 Nail grinder
- 🐾 Fine-tooth comb
- 🐾 Dog specific toothbrush (or finger brush)
- 🐾 Dog toothpaste

BRUSHING

We need to make sure grooming is always a pleasant, fun and mutually enjoyable experience. With that in mind, as soon as you bring your new French Bulldog home, get them used to being handled gently all over. Stroke them gently, making sure you include all four legs, the feet and toes, face, ears, undercarriage, tail and armpits. Before you actually use any grooming tools on your dog, introduce them in a very gentle way – if you just grab a brush and start pulling away at their coats without any warning, then you only have yourself to blame if your dog is a reluctant groomer! Show them the tools, allow them to sniff them and have treats handy to make the connection that when these tools come out, the good times roll!

Once you think your dog is ready for actual grooming,

find a time when your dog is restful. If they've just had a play date and are super-adrenalised, then maybe wait a while.

Start VERY SOFTLY AND SLOWLY – brush gently as if you were stroking your dog with your hand. In these early days, a few minutes at a time is all that is necessary, as we don't want to risk overstepping their tolerance and creating a set-back.

Ensure that you always brush in the direction of the hair. A very common mistake is to only brush the top of the dog, so make sure you go over the whole body. Be careful not to just skim the surface of the coat, but equally, don't be too heavy-handed. Don't apply excessive force that hurts the dog, or they won't want to be groomed in the future. For this reason, be careful not to use a harsh brush.

While grooming your French Bulldog, you will need to check for any potential skin infections, particularly in the skin folds of the face, as well as the ears and any possible small areas on the body (known as 'hotspots'). Many will suffer with a condition known as skin-fold pyoderma – a chronic infection within the folds of skin on the face. It is essential to maintain this area. Specialist wipes, readily available online, used regularly, will simply be your saviour. Gently wipe within the skin folds, disposing of the wipe immediately. Try not to get the skin folds too wet, as this

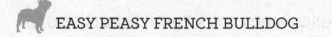

will potentially harbour infection.

French Bulldogs can also suffer with tear staining to their faces. This will be particularly obvious if your dog has a light-coloured coat, but it can occur with any dog. Gently wipe under the eyes daily, starting at the nose. Use cotton wool or a soft tissue dipped in boiled then cooled water.

French Bulldogs do NOT need clipping. This should never be attempted; it can cause 'coat-funk' (which sounds so much cooler than it actually is!), preventing the hair from growing normally and healthily in the future. Shortening the coat does not prevent the dog from shedding dead hair. Be very aware, throughout any groom, that the breed may experience breathing difficulties, particularly if they become stressed. For this reason, make sure that you keep each grooming session short and fun.

It's also worth noting that because the French Bulldog has a short coat, it may be necessary to regularly moisturise the elbows. The gentle application of small amounts of olive oil will help keep the elbows from becoming dry and potentially sore.

Once your dog is used to the idea of being groomed, twice weekly sessions should be sufficient for much of the year, provided that you brush your dog all over.

Grooming regularly allows you to check for foreign bodies in the coat, such as thorns or grass seeds; pay particular attention to between the toes and the pads of the feet, where these can cause infection if not spotted and removed. Grooming will also help you spot fleas or ticks on your dog, although hopefully this will be rare. If you are unsure, use appropriate products recommended by your vet. Grooming will also help you to identify any lumps or bumps on or under the surface of the skin, which might need checking out at the vet.

BATHING

The breed rarely needs a bath – unless they are mud magnets, happiest running through all the slushiest puddles around. If necessary, bathe monthly; you shouldn't need to bathe more frequently than that. Be careful when bathing, as many Frenchies suffer with allergies which can result in skin problems. Make sure that you use an appropriate dog shampoo for sensitive skin (a hypoallergenic shampoo, such as oatmeal, works well) and that you use it in accordance with the manufacturer's instructions. This usually means diluting the shampoo in warm water before applying it to the skin. A hygiene wash of the area underneath the tail is potentially necessary. Use a soft wipe or cloth to gently clean the area. If there are any dried faeces, soften them with lukewarm water first, otherwise they can be painful to remove. Be especially careful not to get shampoo in the eyes as this is painful for the dog, and in the worst cases can cause eye ulcers to form. If, by accident, shampoo goes into the eyes, rinse with copious amounts of <u>lukewarm water.</u>

The easiest way to dry your dog is to use a lovely soft towel to remove as much water as possible and then let the coat dry naturally.

NAILS

Trimming a dog's nails is something many owners are afraid to do. If the nail is cut too short, you could easily catch the 'quick', the fleshy inside of the nail, which bleeds freely if caught and can be very painful for the dog. With dark nails, it is very difficult to accurately judge where the quick is. It is for this reason that nail clipping is often best left to the experts: dog groomers or the vet. An alternative is to use a nail grinder, which gradually files the nails. If you decide to use one, get your dog used to the sensation while they are young, only spending a short time on each nail. Remember: 65% of a dog's body weight is carried on the front legs, so the nails on the front feet grow more quickly than those on the back feet.

To minimise the need for nail clipping, there are simple steps you can take. Ensure you walk your dog on a variety of surfaces: tarmac, gravel, concrete and sand (great excuse for a day at the beach). This variety will help to keep the nails (and quicks within the nails) short. If you only walk on fields, grass or hills, the nails will grow quickly.

Many dogs will have dew claws. These can be on any, some or all four feet and are positioned on the inside of the leg just up from the foot (a bit like a human thumb). Because the dew claw is not in contact with the ground, the nail can grow to a very sharp point or can even curl in on itself and grow into the small pad at its base – for this reason, it is particularly important to keep an eye on dew claws when you are grooming.

EARS

The ears on a French Bulldog are fragile. When you clean them, do so gently using a damp washcloth and make sure you check for any sign of irritation on the inside of the ear flap or within the ear canal (this will show as reddened skin). Do NOT use cotton buds to clean the ears as it is too easy to insert the bud too far into the ear canal or for the bud to fall off into the ear.

TEETH

Eating, drinking and playing tug rope – it's a tough job but someone's gotta do it! Plaque and tartar build-up can create an ideal environment for bacteria to set up home in your dog's mouth leading to smelly breath, infected gums, dental pain or a root abscess. These eventually will lead to a lot of pain and tooth loss. Small breed dogs tend to be more prone to this than larger breeds due to their small mouths and reduced jaw size. So, you need to introduce a dental care routine as early as possible.

Imagine NEVER cleaning your teeth! Horrible thought, isn't it? Yet most dog owners rarely clean their dog's teeth, allowing bacteria, plaque and tartar to build up. In turn, this can cause pain and infection that may require the removal of one, or even many teeth, at an early age.

The key is to start early. Only use pet-specific toothbrushes and toothpaste. Prevent the build-up of plaque and tartar by cleaning your dog's teeth at least every other day. Some dogs may prefer a finger brush to a toothbrush, which is fine. NEVER use human toothpaste – it contains additives that are toxic to dogs.

With puppies, you can start by putting a small amount of puppy toothpaste on your finger and letting your pup lick it off. Then progress to putting your finger in their mouth and running it along the teeth using a circular motion. This will encourage them to get used to the brushing action. Time invested now will literally pay dividends in the future!

If brushing simply isn't an option because the dog wriggles excessively or clamps their mouth shut, then consider giving specific dog dental treats (enzymatic oral hygiene chews), but be aware that these won't be totally effective as dogs simply don't use all their teeth to devour a chew. However, chewing increases saliva and abrasion which helps to remove plaque and prevents it hardening.

Don't be tempted to give an extra-hard chew as an alternative. Products such as whole deer antlers have been known to fracture or excessively wear otherwise healthy teeth. Adding powdered seaweed to your dog's meals can be effective in removing plaque/tartar. Additionally, there are a number of additives you can put into your dog's water which can help maintain good oral health.

NUTRITION

What you feed your French Bulldog is crucial to the health and happiness of your new best friend! I could easily write an entire book on the topic, but for now I have to state the obvious: dogs who are fed a well-balanced and nutritious diet will highly likely enjoy a longer life with less ailments. Same as us! A key part of this is avoiding obesity, so *how much* you feed your dog – not just *what* you feed your dog – is very important. You also need to think about your dog's breed – a small toy breed will be fully grown at six months, whereas a giant breed will not reach full maturity physically until 18–24 months, and sometimes even later. So, tailor the diet to

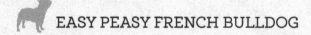

your Frenchie's age, lifestyle and condition.

In this chapter, I will summarise the main dietary options and highlight the pros and cons of each. The whole subject of diet is often very controversial and hotly debated among owners and breeders; there are even veggie dog diets – now there's a conversation starter for you! I think you can see already that if you ask a thousand dog owners about diet, you will get a thousand different views!

With this in mind, we need to avoid being prescriptive, because it is a very personal choice. As long as it's healthy, what choice of food you want for your French Bulldog is entirely up to you.

When considering your dog's diet, you must factor in what stage of life they are at, what breed, what activity level and a number of other elements. For example, dogs who are pregnant or lactating, growing pups, and those who participate in endurance activities require more nutrition (calories, protein, fatty acids) and have other specific nutritional needs. Formulating a balanced diet for these life stages is particularly important as they need specific levels of macronutrients and minerals and too much or too little can lead to problems later in life. A poorly formulated diet can cause health problems at any life stage which can be painful to watch and costly to rectify.

Before I delve into the dog bowl of choice, you need to be aware of the concept of a 'complete' diet, which is the idea that a certain meal contains all the nutrients that your dog will need. In fact, to call itself 'complete', a dog food has to legally prove it contains every nutrient required by a dog for a healthy life.

Alongside 'complete' we have what are known as 'complementary' foods, these are items that do not offer a full complete diet, but are very useful when fed alongside other options – raw meat cuts or chicken wings would be examples.

Finally, we have 'mixer biscuits' which are cereal-based mixes, sometimes with added ingredients such as vegetables or herbs.

Again, at the risk of simplifying a very complex area, how you feed your dog is often split into these choices:

- Kibble/Dry
- Wet
- Raw
- Fresh Complete

DRY

This is the most popular option for the majority of dog owners. Convenient and affordable, the dry diet has been around for years and remains the first choice for many owners and their dogs. You don't need to be an expert in dog dietary requirements, you can safely store this in the home without special treatment and it is available in any pet store or at any online retailer; it is also often competitively priced.

There are a number of ways the food is dried – extrusion, baking, cold-pressed, air-drying, freeze-dried are examples. Dry food has its critics who claim that the diet is too processed and also dull for the dog. The processing in particular is cited as removing many key nutrients from the diet, for example when high temperatures are used in the manufacturing process. Other critics point to added ingredients and query the nutritional value of some of these foods.

WET

Typically sold in a tin or a pouch, this is often the type of diet that many people think of when they talk about dog food. Cooked ingredients are blended and placed in sealed containers for retail, having been heat-sterilised for safe shelf storage. As with dry/kibble, storage is easy and safe, there is a wide and easily accessible choice available and the food requires no expertise on the part of the owner. However, again, critics suggest the higher temperatures used in their manufacture remove nutrients. Fans of wet food say it is a more 'natural' choice than a dry biscuit, that the food has more water and offers the dog a better taste.

RAW

Previously, raw feeding a dog was a very niche choice but in recent times it has started to gain much popularity – helped by many retailers spotting a demand and subsequently offering an ever-wider choice. Many breeders and owners regard this as absolutely the most natural way to feed any dog. There are essentially two ways to raw feed:

- Home-preparation: this is when the owner feeds raw meat but adds specific amounts of ingredients such as bone, offal and vegetable, etc., to create what would be regarded as a 'complete' diet. This is time-intensive and can be pretty complex, and it is very important that the correct dietary balance is achieved for obvious reasons. Owners often make batches of meals and freeze them. However, you do need to be very enthusiastic and meticulous with your preparation. So, if working out the calcium:phosphorus ratio sounds like fun, then homemade raw feeding might be your bag!

- Pre-prepared 'complete' raw meals: this is when a manufacturer has ensured that the product already has a certified balance of nutrients, for example by adding bone powder or vitamins and minerals. This is obviously more convenient than home-prepared raw

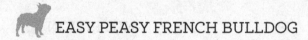

food, although you should note this is almost always supplied frozen.

With both types of raw feeding, great care has to be taken with hygiene – having raw meats in the house needs to be taken very seriously and separate preparation areas from your own food surfaces are needed to avoid contamination and potential illness. Raw meat contains pathogens, so always use good food hygiene practices when handling it. Keep separate utensils, clean every-thing thoroughly and maintain good hand hygiene. Just as with the other types of food, some critics question the nutritional value of raw feeding.

FRESH COMPLETE

This is a relatively new area of dog dietary choice. Essentially, it offers a pre-produced version of home-cooking, often high-end, nutritionally balanced ingred-ients and in a form that is convenient to store and use. Many of the higher end manufacturers only use 'human quality' food (this also applies to top-end raw food). The low levels of processing avoid some of the concerns that are raised over other food types – for example, the lower temperatures used when steaming the ingredients avoids killing off many of the nutrients. Diets can also be tailored to a specific dog's breed, size and preferences – both in terms of nutritional content and also portions.

The lack of preservatives is a plus, but obviously means shelf life is reduced, but against that there are obviously far fewer concerns about handling than with raw food. There is also a growing range to choose from to create home-grown fresh-cooked meals.

Generally, the raw and fresh complete options are perceived as having fewer additives, being less processed and, therefore, more 'natural'. Recent studies have suggested that raw diets and those cooked at low temperatures are more digestible when compared to dry/kibble diets. This is thought to be linked to the quality of ingredients, a lack of processing and the reduced (or no) cooking methods.

Regarding portion size, this really needs to be tailored to your particular dog – for example, it's no good feeding them the same as your neighbour's French Bulldog if that dog is significantly overweight! Remember, just like us, every dog is different.

FOODS TO AVOID

One area all dog owners and breeders can agree on is that certain foods are unsuitable for your dog, and in some cases can be fatal:

🐾 Never feed onion, leeks or any foods from the allium family as these can cause problems with red blood cells.

- Grapes and raisins are nephrotoxic to dogs, meaning they can cause sudden kidney damage.

- Avoid avocados and do not feed macadamia nuts.

- Do not feed corn on the cob – it does not digest well. If your dog swallows large chunks of the cob, or even the whole, it can cause an intestinal blockage due to its size and shape.

- Limit dairy because adult dogs can find it hard to process.

- Avoid cooked bones, as they splinter and can cause injury to the mouth and oesophagus, and cause constipation in the gut.

- Ensure any peanut or nut butters are xylitol free, as this can cause blood sugar crashes, particularly in small breed dogs.

- No chocolate, as the chemical compound in chocolate called theobromine can cause heart rhythm irregularities and even seizures. The type of chocolate, amount and weight of your dog is important. A Pomeranian who has eaten a whole slab of baking chocolate is the worst-case scenario. Pomeranian = light dog. Whole slab = a lot of theobromine. Baking chocolate = very concentrated amount of theobromine. A Labrador who has licked a milk chocolate digestive biscuit is generally less of a concern. Labrador = large dog. Licked = not a lot

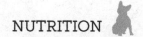

ingested. Milk chocolate = less concentrated amount of theobromine.

What you feed your dog and how much they get is absolutely instrumental to your French Bulldog enjoying a fit, healthy and energetic life – hopefully with less likelihood of ailments and illness. We owe our dogs the care and love to feed them the very best food that we can afford, so have a look at all the options. There is tons of information out there, so get opinions from people that you value and always, always, always consider what is best for your furry pal!

FIRST AID

Let's be honest, French Bulldogs are curious little dogs that love to bound through all sorts of terrain, investigate unknown environments and consequently, with such a lust for life, they're never going to be the most safety-conscious of characters.

Of course, there's no substitute for professional medical care and if you ever have any doubts at all about your dog's health, you should always consult your vet.

However, there may be times when you're in a remote or emergency situation and obviously want to protect your dog from additional pain or suffering – this is where a level of canine first aid knowledge may well come in

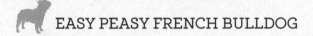

handy.

Where your dog's health is concerned, sooner is always better than later, so let's note a few basic health signs to look out for with your French Bulldog:

Ears: Should be clean without any wax or discharge. No redness, itchiness or offensive smell. Believe me, you will know it when you smell it!

Eyes: Should be bright and clear, no sign of runniness, redness or soreness. Your dog shouldn't squint or shy away from bright light.

Nose: No crusting, runniness or thickened discharge.

Mouth: Teeth should be clean with no excessive thick, brown tartar. Gums should be a healthy pink (or black, depending on skin pigmentation) and not red, swollen or bleeding. Look out for a reluctance to eat, excessive salivation, clawing at the mouth or bad breath as a sign of mouth problems.

Skin and Coat: The coat should be free of crusting, itching, scaling, spots, infected or hot and inflamed areas. It should be shiny with no broken hairs, bald patches or dandruff. No lumps, bumps or tenderness to touch.

Nails: These should be smooth and can be either white or black. Nails that are roughened and flake or break easily may require veterinary attention. When checking your dog's nails, don't forget to check their dew claws - this is the additional nail high on your dog's wrist.

Paws: Check pads and between toes - there should be no swelling, flaking, cracks, redness or excess heat.

Digestion: Keep an eye on your dog's appetite and always know what you are feeding and what everyone else in the family may be feeding. Frenchies famously have a very heathy appetite(!) so it should be easy to spot any concerns. There should be no vomiting, reluctance to eat or difficulty experienced when eating. Stools should be a consistent brown colour and of solid texture, without any straining, blood or mucus (clear jelly) passed.

Thirst: If your dog suddenly becomes very thirsty or starts drinking more than usual without excessive exercise, it can indicate an underlying medical problem and you should consult your vet.

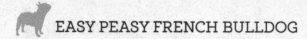

Attitude: As they tend to wear their heart on their sleeve, your Frenchie's general attitude can tell you a lot. If you notice the head and tail are down and they seem quieter, are maybe less playful than usual, skulking in corners or sometimes appear unusually aggressive for no apparent reason, or if you notice any other unusual changes, always ask your vet for advice.

Capillary Refill Time (CRT): This is observed by pressing your finger on the surface of your dog's gum line until there is no colour beneath your finger. When you remove the pressure, the colour should resurface within one to two seconds. A slow refill can indicate heart disease or other medical condition which affects blood flow. A slow refill may suggest shock, a fast fill may indicate high blood pressure. If your dog has an accelerated or reduced refill time, seek veterinary advice.

These are the basic areas you should always be aware of, and to help you take action should you spot any concerns, it's always worth having access to a basic canine first aid kit. Maybe have one in your car and a second one that you can wear around your waist should you and your dog decide to go on a long hike together.

First Aid Kit

Towel	Bandages
Tweezers	Vet wrap
Saline solution	Safety pins
Rubber gloves	Whistle (to call for help)
Scissors	Emergency blanket

Talking about long hikes, often you may be away from your home with your dog, perhaps on a special day trip or holiday. Wherever you are, please keep a note of your *local* emergency veterinary service.

Okay, let's imagine your French Bulldog is in some kind of physical distress and, of course, you want to minimise any suffering you can before getting them to the vet. First thing's first, assess the environment:

Is the environment safe for you?
Look out for hazards, such as:
- 🐾 Electricity
- 🐾 Slip hazards
- 🐾 Chemicals
- 🐾 Traffic
- 🐾 Dog bite

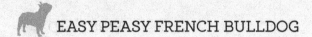

Can you get help from ...?

- Passers-by
- Emergency vet

Check for vital signs

- The ABC:

    - Airway: Is the airway clear?

    - Breathing: Ideally 24 to 42 breaths per second

    - Circulation: Pulse should be 60 to 160 beats per second

- Temperature: 38 to 39.2°C

- Hydration: Pick up the skin between the fingers. It should return to its normal position quickly. If not, this may indicate dehydration. Also feel the gums because dry, sticky gums can also indicate dehydration or heat stroke.

If you are unsure of the *cause* of your dog's distress, perform a quick body scan. Check for:

- *Ears*: Cuts

- *Eyes*: Clarity, whiteness, debris, scratches

- *Nose*: Blood, discharge

- *Mouth*: Injuries to teeth or tongue, signs of foreign bodies. Also, check your dog's inner cheeks and gums, known as the mucous membranes:

- Pink = normal

- Pale or blue = shock, blood loss

- Red = High blood pressure, heat stroke, poisoning

- Yellow = jaundice (liver damage)

- *Head*: Injuries, foreign body, swelling

- *Neck*: Injuries, signs of discomfort/tenderness to touch

- *Skeletal structure and skin*: Misshapen bones, lumps/bumps along bone line, tenderness to touch, cuts, bruising (or any discolouration), foreign body, signs of irritation

- *Limbs (including shoulders/hips)*: Misshapen joints, swelling, heat, tenderness to touch

- *Paws (check pads, toes, claws)*: Cuts, tears, foreign body, signs of burning, tenderness to touch

- *Tail*: Misshapen, slight kinks, tenderness to touch

GDV/BLOAT GDV
(GASTRIC DILATATION AND VOLVULUS)

Also known as Gastric Torsion, GDV is a life-threatening condition in which the stomach distends with gas and twists (torsion). In some cases, the stomach merely distends with gas and does not twist (bloat). It is uncertain exactly what causes GDV, but it is most commonly seen two to three hours following ingestion of a meal, particularly if

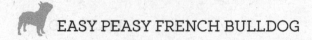

eating follows strenuous exercise or after drinking a large amount of water.

What to look for

- 🐾 Distended abdomen
- 🐾 Unsuccessful attempts to belch or vomit
- 🐾 Retching without producing anything
- 🐾 Weakness
- 🐾 Excessive salivation
- 🐾 Shortness of breath
- 🐾 Cold body temperature
- 🐾 Pale gums
- 🐾 Rapid heartbeat
- 🐾 Collapse

If your dog shows any symptoms of GDV/Bloat call the emergency vet <u>immediately</u>.

EYE INJURIES

There are three main types of eye trauma:

1. Surface trauma – foreign body on the surface of the eye

- 🐾 Try to keep the dog calm.
- 🐾 Do not force the eyelid open.
- 🐾 Do not try to remove the object by hand.

- Use saline solution to flush out the object (saline does not affect the pH balance of the eye). In the absence of saline, use cold water and flush from the inside outwards. If the dog shows any signs of irritation, redness or swelling, take them to the vet as soon as possible.

2. *Penetrating trauma into the eye*
   - Try to keep the dog calm.
   - Do not force the eyelid open.
   - Do not try to remove any foreign body by hand (it may be a protruding part of the eye itself).
   - If the injury is preventing the dog from closing its eye, you will need to keep it moist with KY jelly or a damp cloth. You will also need to prevent the dog from clawing at it.
   - Seek emergency veterinary assistance.

3. *Prolapse of the eye – when the eye leaves the eye socket*
   - Keep the area moist with KY jelly or a damp cloth.
   - Prevent the dog from clawing at it.
   - Seek emergency veterinary assistance **immediately.**
   - Do not try to replace the eye back in the socket.

SHOCK

Shock is a life-threatening medical condition in which the dog's body has an inadequate flow of oxygenated blood to the body's tissues, which can cause major damage to organs. A dog in shock needs to get medical help immediately, as shock can worsen rapidly and may result in death.

Potential causes of shock
- 🐾 Injury
- 🐾 Body trauma
- 🐾 Dehydration
- 🐾 Poisoning
- 🐾 Heat stroke
- 🐾 Submersion

What to look for
- 🐾 Lethargy/weakness
- 🐾 Shallow, rapid breathing
- 🐾 Rapid, weak, difficult to find pulse
- 🐾 Cold limbs/tail
- 🐾 Glazed eyes
- 🐾 Unconsciousness
- 🐾 Low body temperature

The gums/mucous membranes can be indicators of shock:
- 🐾 Early stages – bright red
- 🐾 Mid stages – pale or blue
- 🐾 Late stages – white or mottled

How to Help

1. Check the ABC (as listed on page 148) – Airway, Breathing, Circulation.
2. Stop/reduce blood loss.
3. Protect fractures/injured joint.
4. Prevent loss of body heat.
5. Position so that the legs are slightly elevated.
6. Contact and transport to vet immediately.

INSECT STINGS

First question: is the sting still in the skin?

If so, **DO NOT REMOVE WITH TWEEZERS** as this can inject more discomfort into the area. Instead, gently squeeze the sting out by pushing the flesh around it or remove it with a hard-edged object, such as a credit card.

How to Help

Bee – use bicarbonate of soda mixed into a watery paste.

Wasp – use vinegar or lemon juice to relieve the pain.

An easy way to remember is 'bicarb for bees and winegar for wasps'.

HEAT STROKE

Heat stroke is caused by exposure to extreme heat and can

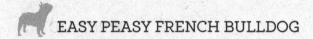

lead to organ failure and death. It can be caused by situations such as:

- Being left in a hot car
- Over-exercising on a hot, sunny day
- Lying in the sun for long periods of time

Dogs with thick coats and short muzzles/narrow airways are at higher risk of heat stroke. Moderate heat stroke is classified as a temperature of over 104°F/40°C. Severe heat stroke is classified as a temperature of over 106°F/41°C.

What to look for

- Dry, sticky gums
- Excessive panting
- Restlessness
- Excessive drooling
- Vomiting
- Loss of consciousness

How to Help

1. Cool the dog down by placing cold, wet towels over them.
2. Offer the dog cool water to drink.
3. Call your vet for advice **immediately**.

CHOKING

Firstly, use both hands to open the mouth, with one hand on the upper jaw and the other pushing down on the lower. Grasping the jaws, press the lips over the dog's teeth so that they are between the teeth and your fingers. Look inside the mouth and remove the obstruction with your fingers if you can. If there are two of you, one of you should hold your dog's mouth open and the other look inside. If you can't move the object with your fingers, use a flat spoon handle to pry it away from the teeth or roof of the mouth.

Secondly, place your arm under the dog's abdomen and raise their hind legs so that their head is pointed down. Give them up to five sharp blows between the shoulder blades with the heel of your hand.

Lastly, if nothing else helps and your dog cannot breathe, you might consider performing the Heimlich manoeuvre. Only use this if you are certain your dog is choking on a foreign object, as it can cause additional injury. To do this:

Place your arm around the dog's waist. Ensure that your dog's head points down. Form a fist and bring your other hand around and cover your fist with it. Your two-handed fist should be placed between the dog's abdomen and its ribcage (specifically the soft spot just under the ribcage). The size of the dog will affect the exact positioning of your hands.

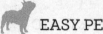

If you have a puppy, you may want to use two fingers with the same amount of force so you do not damage your dog's ribcage.

Quickly and firmly give three to five thrusts inwards and upwards. Repeat as often as is necessary to dislodge whatever is blocking your dog's airway.

If the dog is lying down, place one hand on the back for support and use the other hand to squeeze the abdomen upwards and forwards.

BURNS AND SCALDS

Burns can be caused by a variety of household items, including electrical equipment and chemicals. They can cause deep damage and shock, sometimes days after the accident. Burns are primarily caused by one of three things:

- chemicals
- electricity
- heat from liquids or hot objects

It is essential to quickly ascertain the cause of the burn so that it can be appropriately treated.

How to Help
Chemical burns

Wearing rubber gloves to avoid being burned yourself, remove any contaminated collars or harness. Flush the affected area with cold water for 20 minutes, making sure you don't spread the chemicals and burn other areas. Once flushed with water, cover superficial burns with a non-stick bandage and contact your vet for advice on further treatment.

Burns from liquids or hot objects

Cool the burned area as quickly and for as long as possible. You can do this with a gentle stream of cool water. The quicker you cool the area, the less damage will be done.

Once the area has been flushed with water, apply a cold compress for 20 minutes – using something like a bag of frozen vegetables over a non-stick pad. Contact your vet for advice on further treatment.

Electrical burns

Burns from electrical equipment or power cords can be treated in the same way as liquids or hot objects. However, before touching the dog or surrounding cables, make sure the electricity is turned off and unplug the equipment.

BLEEDING

With a bleeding injury, the main purpose of any first aid is to prevent excessive blood loss, which can lead to shock. As little as two teaspoons of blood loss per pound of body weight can result in shock.

There are two types of bleed:

- 🐾 Arterial – bright red and spraying
- 🐾 Vein/small vessel – burgundy and seeping

Treatment

Direct pressure on a wound is the most preferable way to stop bleeding. Gently press a pad of clean cloth or gauze over the bleeding area; this will absorb the blood and allow a clot to form. If blood soaks through, do not remove the pad as this will disrupt the clot. Add additional layers of cloth and continue the direct pressure more evenly. If you don't have cloth or gauze, you can apply pressure with a bare hand or finger. Once bleeding is under control, the compress can be bandaged in place and the dog can be transported to a vet. If a severely bleeding wound is on a limb, and there is no evidence of a broken bone, gently elevate the limb so that the wound is above the level of the heart.

Direct pressure on the wound must be continued in

addition to elevation.

Elevation uses the force of gravity to help reduce blood pressure in the injured area, slowing the bleeding.

Arterial pressure

In extreme cases when bleeding continues after you have used direct pressure and elevation and the dog is at high risk of bleeding to death, you can use your finger or thumb to place pressure over the main artery to the wound. In this case, the dog must not be moved and an emergency vet must be called.

Wow! All of that sounds pretty horrific, I know, and, of course, we all hope that you never have to experience any of the above, but if you do, at least you'll be prepared.

Good preparation and regular checks should help you avoid as many emergencies as possible with your dog; however, you may be out walking and come across someone else's dog that could appreciate your first aid support. These are fantastic skills to have in your armoury as a dog owner and dog lover.

Final reminder: if in doubt, *always* call your vet. Better safe than sorry!

A FINAL WORD

So, there you have it!

I wish you and your Frenchie (or Frencheaux, if you've really got the bug!) a wonderful life together, full of love and adventures that'll provide you with memories forever.

Remember – *serious teacher's face* – play the cards you're dealt. You'd be crazy to fight against your dog's innate spirit and super-hero skills to use their nose, to love interacting with people and to seek out fun and joy in every situation.

Look for opportunities to use what your *dog* loves to reinforce the behaviours *you* love. Dog training isn't about you versus your dog. Good dog training should always feel like the perfect negotiation, in which both parties are happy and looking forward to the next stage of learning, together. If it ever feels tough, drop me a line, I'll point you in the right direction.

Finally, I want you to do one thing for me...

... play with your dog, every day.

Play will bring you and your French Bulldog to a happy and healthy place that is too special to ignore. If you and your Frenchie enjoy being in each other's company, then everything else instantly becomes easier. I promise!

Steve Mann

APPENDIX

The Hounds For Heroes Charity
Created by Allen Parton and inspired by his special relationship with the legendary Labrador, Endal, the charity states that, 'Our mission is to provide specially trained assistance dogs to injured and disabled men and women of both the UK Armed Forces and Emergency Services. We aim to provide help and practical support leading to an enhanced quality of life.'

For more information, please visit:
www.houndsforheroes.com

ACKNOWLEDGEMENTS

With special thanks to all the dogs that continue to teach me, (I know they can't read this which may make it look like an empty gesture, but a lot of them listen to audio books).

Also muchas gracias to Martin Roach who insists I keep writing to earn my freedom, and to Matt Phillips and Madiya Altaf for looking after me at Bonnier Books UK.

INDEX

EVEN MORE FROM STEVE MANN

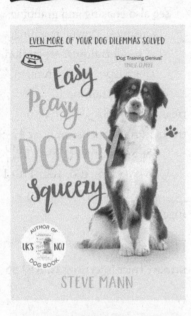
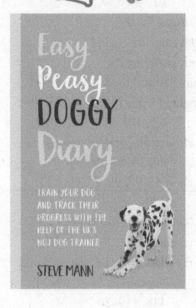

Printed in the USA
CPSIA information can be obtained
at www.ICGtesting.com
JSHW031624060924
69387JS00007B/23